THE CONCEPT OF THE POLITICAL

CARL SCHMITT

Translation, Introduction, and Notes by George Schwab
With Leo Strauss's Notes on Schmitt's Essay,
   Translated by J. Harvey Lomax
Foreword by Tracy B. Strong

THE UNIVERSITY OF CHICAGO PRESS
Chicago and London

The University of Chicago Press, Chicago 60637
The University of Chicago Press, Ltd., London
© 1996 by The University of Chicago
All rights reserved.
University of Chicago Press edition 1996
Printed in the United States of America
14 13 12 11 10 09 08 07 06 05   6 7 8 9 10
ISBN: 0-226-73886-8 (paper)

Library of Congress Cataloging-in-Publication Data

Schmitt, Carl, 1888–
    [Begriff des Politischen. English]
    The concept of the political / Carl Schmitt ; translation, introduction, and notes by George Schwab ; with Leo Strauss's notes on Schmitt's essay ; translated by J. Harvey Lomax ; foreword by Tracy B. Strong.
       p.   cm.
    Includes index.
    1. Political science.   2. State, The.   I. Title.
JA74.S313   1996
320'.01'1—dc20   95-44342
                                              CIP

THE CONCEPT OF THE POLITICAL

To Edward Rosen
Inspiring Teacher, Devoted Friend

CONTENTS

FOREWORD: DIMENSIONS OF THE NEW DEBATE AROUND CARL SCHMITT

Tracy B. Strong

> *"What did they live on,"* said Alice, who always took a great interest
> in questions of eating and drinking. *"They lived on treacle,"* said the
> Dormouse, after thinking a moment or two. *"They couldn't have done
> that, you know,"* Alice gently remarked. *"They'd have been ill."*
> *"So they were,"* said the Dormouse, *"very ill."*
>
> Lewis Carroll, Alice in Wonderland

> *The philosopher's every attempt at directly influencing the tyrant is
> necessarily ineffectual.*
>
> Alexandre Kojève, Tyranny and Wisdom[1]

Carl Schmitt was a prominent legal scholar in post–World War I Germany and one of the leading intellectuals during the Weimar period. Exceptionally active as a teacher and publicist, he probed the nature and sources of what he took to be the weakness of the modern liberal, parliamentary state, both in its embodiment in the Weimar constitution and more broadly as the modern form of political organization. He joined the Nazi Party in 1933 (in May, the same month as did Martin Heidegger) and published

---

[1] In Victor Gourevitch and Michael Roth, eds., Leo Strauss, *On Tyranny: Including the Strauss-Kojève Debate* (New York: Free Press, 1991), pp. 165–166.

several works, some of them anti-Semitic, in which he explicitly defended the policies of the regime. (He would later claim that he was trying to give his own understanding of Nazi ideas.)[2] In 1936 he was severely criticized in articles published in *Das Schwarze Korps,* an official SS organ. Protected by Herman Göring, he remained in his post at the University of Berlin and continued teaching and writing but with a much reduced focus on contemporary domestic German matters. He was detained for an eighteen-month period after the war by Allied authorities, but never formally charged with crimes. He never resumed a university position. Festschriften were published on the occasions of his seventieth and eightieth birthdays; among the authors contributing were Julien Freund, Reinhart Koselleck, and Karlfried Gründer. He died in 1985 at the age of ninety-six.

From the beginning of his career, Schmitt was taken seriously on all parts of the political spectrum. The young Carl Friedrich (later to become a central author of the postwar German constitution, a Harvard professor, and president of the American Political Science Association) cited him approvingly, in 1930, on Article 48 of the Weimar constitution, which permitted commissarial dictatorship, a step that Schmitt had urged on Hindenberg.[3] Franz Neumann, the socialist and left-wing sociologist author of *Behemoth,* drew extensively upon Schmitt, as did his colleague and friend Otto Kirchheimer.[4] Indeed, all of the Frankfurt School

[2] See the transcript of his interrogation after the war in Joseph W. Bendersky, "Schmitt at Nuremberg," *Telos* 72 (Summer 1987), pp. 106–107. The standard English biography (quite sympathetic), also by Bendersky, is *Carl Schmitt: Theorist for the Reich* (Princeton: Princeton University Press, 1983).

[3] C. J. Friedrich, "Dictatorship in Germany?" *Foreign Affairs* 9, no. 1 (October 1930). It is worth noting that most of those who defend or apologize for Schmitt pull out a long list of those who have cited him favorably.

[4] For a somewhat sensationalist but still revealing discussion of the changes in attitudes by left-wing scholars to Schmitt, see George Schwab, "Carl Schmitt: Through a Glass Darkly," *Eclectica* 17 (1988), pp. 71–72. I owe this reference to Paul Edward Gottfried, *Carl Schmitt: Politics and Theory* (New York: Greenwood Press, 1990), p. 126.

(especially Walter Benjamin) spoke highly of him, often after 1933.[5] More recently, the Italian and French Left, as well as those associated with the radical journal *Telos,* have approvingly investigated his nonideological conception of the political.[6] The European Right, as well as American conservatives of a Straussian persuasion, find in his work at least the beginnings of a theory of authority that might address the supposed failings of individualistic liberalism. Just as interestingly, a number of defenders of liberalism have found it necessary to single out Schmitt for attack,[7] a need they

[5] See Samuel Weber, "Taking Exception to Decision: Walter Benjamin and Carl Schmitt," *diacritics* 22, nos. 3–4 (Fall-Winter 1992), pp. 5–18. A controversy around this and other issues was set off by Ellen Kennedy, "Carl Schmitt and the Frankfurt School," *Telos* 71 (Spring 1987), pp. 37–66, and the responses from Martin Jay, Alfons Söllner, and Ulrich Preuss that follow in the same issue. Kennedy's rejoinder appears in the Fall 1987 issue. It appears fairly obvious that Kennedy has successfully established the debt owed by most members of the Frankfurt School, including Habermas, to Schmitt.

[6] As Stephen Holmes caustically remarks, the editors of *Telos* spoke of learning *from*, not *about*, Carl Schmitt. See Stephen Holmes, *The Anatomy of Antiliberalism* (Cambridge: Harvard University Press, 1993), p. 37. The reference is to Paul Piccone and G. L. Ulmen, "Introduction to Carl Schmitt," *Telos* 72 (Summer 1987), p. 14.

[7] Stephen Holmes, as far back as 1983, spoke in a review of Bendersky's biography of Schmitt as a man "who consciously embraced evil." *American Political Science Review* 77, no. 3 (September, 1983), p. 1067. He devotes a nasty chapter to Schmitt in *The Anatomy of Antiliberalism*. Richard Bellamy and Peter Baehr devote over twenty pages to Schmitt only to find his work "unconvincing." "Carl Schmitt and the Contradictions of Liberal Democracy," *European Journal of Political Research* 23 (1993), pp. 163–185. Giovanni Sartori, in a contribution to the initial issue of the *Journal of Theoretical Politics* ("The Essence of the Political in Carl Schmitt," 1, no. 1 [1989], pp. 64–75), feels the need to defend a more peaceful conception of politics against that which he finds in Schmitt. Jürgen Habermas, in "The Horrors of Autonomy: Carl Schmitt in English," *The New Conservatism* (Cambridge: MIT Press, 1992, pp. 128–139) links Schmitt to the French and English-language postmodernists whom he detests, as well as to those in Germany who seek to find a continuity in German history. Habermas, "Le besoin d'une continuité allemande: Carl Schmitt dans l'histoire des idées politiques de la RFA," *Les temps modernes*, no. 575 (June 1994), pp. 26–35. More

do not feel with other critics of liberal parliamentarism who were members of the Nazi Party. By virtue of the range of those to whom he appeals and the depth of his political allegiance during the Nazi era, Schmitt comes close these days to being the Martin Heidegger of political theory.[8]

I cannot here do more than to call attention to these facts.[9] If a definition of an important thinker is to have a manifold of supporters and detractors,[10] the scholars I have cited clearly show Schmitt a thinker to be taken seriously. This is new. Entries in the standard reference work, *The Blackwell Encyclopedia of Political Thought,* published in 1987, go from "Schiller, Friedrich" to "Schumpeter, Joseph." No Carl Schmitt. Yet recent years have seen an explosion of work on Schmitt, in English-speaking countries as well as in Germany.[11] A question thus accompanies the welcome

---

sympathetic, Chantal Mouffe finds him "an adversary as rigorous as he is insightful," in "Penser la démocratie moderne avec, et contre, Carl Schmitt," *Revue française de science politique* 42, no. 1 (February 1992), p. 83. A computer search of the holdings of a research university library on Schmitt comes up with sixty-three journal articles in the last five years as well as thirty-six books published since 1980, most of them since 1990. By comparison, the search reveals 164 articles on Heidegger, and twenty-six on Hitler.

[8] Around the time they both joined the Nazi Party, Schmitt initiated contact with Heidegger by sending him a copy of *The Concept of the Political.* Heidegger responded warmly and indicated that he hoped Schmitt would assist him in "reconstituting the Law Faculty." This letter appears on p. 132 of the *Telos* issue cited above. Schmitt, Heidegger, and Bäumler were the three most prominent German intellectuals to join the party.

[9] Accounts of it may be found in the excellent Gottfried, *Carl Schmitt,* chaps. 1 and 5; George Schwab, *The Challenge of the Exception,* 2d ed. (New York: Greenwood Press, 1989), Conclusion; Arnim Mohler, "Schmittistes de droite, Schmittistes de gauche, et Schmittistes établis," *Nouvelle ecole* 44 (Spring 1987), pp. 29–66.

[10] For this argument see my *Jean-Jacques Rousseau: The Politics of the Ordinary* (SAGE, 1994), chap. 1.

[11] MIT Press has brought out in recent years translations of *Political Theology* (1985), *The Crisis of Parliamentary Democracy* (1986), and *Political Romanticism* (1986).

reissuing of Schmitt's *The Concept of the Political*. What is the significance of the rebirth of interest in Schmitt, a leading conservative jurist during the Weimar Republic, a scholar severely compromised by his participation in and support for the Nazi regime? Why is he now a focus for contention? What do we learn about our intellectual interests and problems in the attention now being paid to Carl Schmitt?

The intense and renewed attention to the work of Carl Schmitt, whether hostile or favorable, is due to the fact that he sits at the intersection of three central questions which any contemporary political theorist must consider. The first is the relation between liberalism and democracy. The second is the relation between politics and ethics. The third is the importance of what Schmitt called "enemies" for state legitimation and the implication of that importance for the relation between domestic and international politics. His understandings of these questions raise a final issue, which quietly frames all of the others; it has to do with the nature and consequence of the growing distance between the contemporary world and the events associated with the advent of Nazism. I want here to examine each of the questions, both substantively and in terms of their interest and challenge to the various schools of thought that take Schmitt seriously. I am going to call these schools "left," "right," and "liberal." I do so with the recognition that these terms may be outmoded and even a source of confusion in our world.

The Relation between Liberalism and Democracy

Schmitt's conception of the political stands in opposition to his conception of "political romanticism," the subject of one of his early books. Political romanticism is characterized as a stance of occasionalist ironism, such that there is no last word on anything. Political romanticism is the doctrine of the autonomous, isolated, and solitary individual, whose absolute stance toward himself gives a world in which nothing is connecting to anything else. Political romanticism is thus at the root of what Schmitt sees as the liberal tendency to substitute perpetual discussion for the political.[12] On the positive side, Schmitt's conception of the political stands in alliance with the subject of his subsequent book, *Political Theology.* There he elaborates a conception of sovereignty as the making of decisions which concern the exception.[13] The political is the arena of authority rather than general law and requires decisions which are singular, absolute and final.[14] Thus, as Schmitt notes in *Political Theology,* the sovereign decision has the quality of being something like a religious miracle: it has no references except the fact that it is, to what Heidegger would have called its *Dasein.* (It should be noted that the sovereign is not like God: there *is* no "Sovereign." Rather, sovereign acts have the quality of referring only to themselves, as moments of "existential intervention.")[15]

This is, for Schmitt, a given quality of "the political." What distresses him is that the historical conjunction of liberalism and democracy has obscured this conception, such that we are in danger of losing the experience of the political. In *The Concept of the Political* Schmitt identifies this loss of the conception of the political with the triumph of the modern notion of politics, dating loosely from the French Revolution but already present in seventeenth-century doctrines such as those of Cardinal Bellarmine, whose theory of indirect powers Hobbes went to extended pains to attack in chapter 41 of *Leviathan.* Politics thus involves, famously, friends

---

[12] See *The Concept of the Political* (henceforth CP), below, p. 71.

[13] Cf Karl Löwith, "Le décisionisme (occasionnel) de Carl Schmitt," *Les temps modernes,* no. 544 (November 1991), pp. 15–50. The publishing history of Löwith's text is given on page 15.

[14] For a discussion of the influence of Kierkegaard on Schmitt, see Löwith, ibid., pp. 19–21.

[15] See Ellen Kennedy, "Carl Schmitt and the Frankfurt School: A Rejoinder," *Telos* 73 (Fall 1987), pp. 105, 107.

and enemies, which means at least the centrality of those who are with you and those against whom you struggle. Fighting and the possibility of death are necessary for there to be the political.[16]

From this standpoint, Schmitt came to the following conclusions about modern bourgeois politics. First, it is a system which rests on compromise; hence all of its solutions are in the end temporary, occasional, never decisive. Second, such arrangements can never resolve the claims of equality inherent in democracy. By the universalism implicit in its claims for equality, democracy challenges the legitimacy of the political order, as liberal legitimacy rests on discussion and the compromise of shifting majority rules. Third, liberalism will tend to undermine the possibility of the political in that it wishes to substitute procedure for struggle. Thus, last, legitimacy and legality cannot be the same; indeed, they stand in contradiction to each other.[17]

The driving force behind this argument lies in its claim that politics cannot be made safe and that the attempt to make politics safe will result in the abandonment of the state to private interests and to "society." The reality of an empirical referent for this claim was undeniable in the experience of Weimar. (It is worth remembering that Schmitt was among those who sought to strengthen the Weimar regime by trying to persuade Hindenburg to invoke the temporary dictatorial powers of article 48 against the extremes on the Right and the Left.)[18]

There is here, however, a deeper claim, a claim that the political defines what it is to be a human being in the modern world and that those who would diminish the political diminish humanity. Schmitt lays this out as the "friend-enemy" distinction. What is important about this distinction is not so much the "who

---

[16] CP 35.

[17] I have loosely followed here the excellent analysis in Kennedy, *Telos* 71, p. 42.

[18] As Paul Piccone and G. L. Ulmen point out to Jeffrey Herf in "Reading and Misreading Schmitt," *Telos* 74 (Winter 1987–88), pp. 133–140.

is on my side" quality, but the claim that only by means of this distinction does the question of our willingness to take responsibility for *our own* lives arise. "Each participant is in a position to judge whether the adversary intends to negate his opponent's way of life and therefore must be repulsed or fought *in order to preserve one's own form of existence.*"[19] It is this quality that attracts the nonliberal Left and the Right to Schmitt. It is precisely to deny that the stakes of politics should be so high that liberals resist Schmitt. If a liberal is a person who cannot take his own side in an argument, a liberal is also a person who, as Schmitt notes, thereby raising the stakes, if asked "'Christ or Barabbas?' [responds] with a proposal to adjourn or appoint a committee of investigation."[20]

The Relation between Politics and Ethics

Schmitt claimed that liberalism's reliance on procedure led to a depoliticization and dehumanization of the world. It was the daring of the claim for the political that drew Leo Strauss's attention in the critique he wrote of *The Concept of the Political* in 1932. Schmitt had written: "The political adversaries of a clear political theory will . . . easily refute political phenomena and truths in the name of some autonomous discipline as amoral, uneconomical, unscientific and above all declare this—and this is politically relevant—a devilry worthy of being combated."[21] Schmitt's claim was not just that the political was a separate realm of human activity, parallel to ethics, economics, science, and religion, but that inquiry

---

[19] CP 27 (my italics).

[20] Carl Schmitt, *The Crisis of Parliamentary Democracy* (Cambridge: MIT Press, 1985), p. 62.

[21] CP 65–66.

into the political was an inquiry into the "order of human things," where the important word is "human."[22]

To claim this was to claim that the possibility of dying for what one was was the final determining quality of the human. Schmitt's existential Hobbesianism thus saw moral claims as implicitly denying the finality of death in favor of an abstract universalism in which human beings were not particularly involved in what they were. As Herbert Marcuse noted, "Carl Schmitt inquires into the reason for such sacrifice: 'There is no rational end, no norm however correct, no program however exemplary, no social ideal however beautiful, and no legitimacy or legality that could justify men's killing one another.' What, then, remains as a possible justification? Only this: that there is a state of affairs that through its very existence and presence is exempt from all justification, i.e. an 'existential,' 'ontological' state of affairs,—justification by mere existence."[23] It is this quality in Schmitt that is at the basis of the accusations of irrationalism and decisionism.[24]

Two questions are at stake here. The first is whether it is possible to escape the hold of an ethical universalism; the second is that if it is possible, where then does one find oneself—what does it mean to go "beyond good and evil"? Schmitt clearly thought that he had given a positive answer to the first question: that people will only be responsible for what they are if the reality of death and conflict remain present.[25] Such considerations transcend the

---

[22] Leo Strauss, Notes on Carl Schmitt, *The Concept of the Political* (henceforth NCP), below, par. 1.

[23] Herbert Marcuse, *Negations* (Boston: Beacon, 1968), pp. 30–31. Martin Jay, quite unfairly, adduces this essay to claim against Ellen Kennedy that Marcuse was fundamentally hostile to Schmitt. See note 5 above.

[24] Richard Wolin extends Habermas's critique and claims that Schmitt's critique of liberalism has "its basis in the vitalist critique of Enlightenment rationalism." ("Carl Schmitt, the Conservative Revolutionary: Habitus and the Aesthetics of Horror," *Political Theory* 20, no. 3 (August 1992), pp. 424–447, at 432.

[25] CP 77. For an exploration of the relation of Schmitt to Max Weber on

ethical and place one—this is Schmitt's answer to the second question—in the realm of nature. As Strauss notes: "Schmitt returns,
contrary to liberalism, to its author, Hobbes, in order to strike at
the root of liberalism in Hobbes's express negation of the state of
nature."[26]

However, as Strauss brilliantly shows, it is highly contestable
that Schmitt actually has achieved what he believes himself to have
accomplished. Strauss demonstrates that Schmitt remains concerned with the *meaningfulness* of life—he is afraid that modernity
will make life unmeaningful. He thus, as Strauss concludes, remains within the horizon of liberal moralist. "The affirmation of
the political," writes Strauss, "is ultimately nothing other than
the affirmation of the moral."[27] Schmitt has, albeit unwillingly,
moralized even his would-be amorality.

It is out of the scope of this foreword to indicate how Schmitt
might have done otherwise. Strauss indicates that Schmitt has
merely prepared the way for a radical critique of liberalism. However, Schmitt "is tying himself to his opponents' view of morality
instead of questioning the claim of humanitarian-pacifist morality
to *be* morals; he remains trapped in the view that he is attacking."[28]
It is important to note that the nature of Strauss's critique of
Schmitt indicates that whatever his own critique of liberalism will
be, it cannot be a simple reaffirmation of moral truths. Rather
(and all too gnomically) "IT IS TO UNDERSTAND SOCRATES," as the
highlighted words beginning the Introduction and chapters 3 and
4 of Strauss's *Natural Right and History* (a book overtly about
liberalism and not Socrates) let us know.[29] One should also note

---

these matters, see W. J. Mommsen, *Max Weber and German Politics,* 1890–1920
(Chicago: University of Chicago Press, 1984), esp. pp. 389 ff.

[26] NCP, par. 14.

[27] NCP, par. 27.

[28] NCP, par. 30.

[29] On these matters see the excellent book by Heinrich Meier, *Carl Schmitt
and Leo Strauss* (Chicago: University of Chicago Press, 1995), esp. p. 86. The

here, as Heinrich Meier points out, that Schmitt never engaged in a full-fledged confrontation with Nietzsche.[30] To some of those on the Left, Schmitt's according of primacy to the political thus appears to open the door to a kind of postmodernism.[31] Here, his insistence on the centrality of antagonistic relations and his resistance to an abstract, not to say "thin," understanding of agency fit in well with those who see liberalism as a historical event. To see liberalism as a historical event means that one understands it as the inheritor and bearer not only of rights and freedoms but also of structures of power and domination, of colonial and class exploitations, of the hatred of, rather than the opposition to, the Other.[32] Such a response to Schmitt is, however, a highly selective choice of some elements of his doctrine. It tacitly introduces elements of democracy by pluralizing his notion of sovereignty and suggesting that the decision about the exception is a decision that *each* person can make. It is to claim that value-pluralism is not inherently undesirable.[33] Against this one can insist that Schmitt,

---

other chapters in *Natural Right and History* all begin with the word "The." For a critique of the Strauss critique of Schmitt, see John P. McCormick, "Fear, Technology, and the State: Carl Schmitt, Leo Strauss, and the Revival of Hobbes in Weimar and National Socialist Germany," *Political Theory* 22, no. 4 (November 1994), pp. 619–652.

[30] See Meier, *Carl Schmitt and Leo Strauss*, p. 65, n. 72. Wolin, *Political Theory* 20, no. 3, finds strongly Nietzschean elements in Schmitt. However, the elements that he finds are simply the same ones that he dislikes in Schmitt.

[31] See Piccone and Ulmen, *Telos* 74, p. 138.

[32] See William Connolly, "Beyond Good and Evil: The Ethical Sensibility of Michel Foucault," *Political Theory* 21, no. 3 (August 1993), pp. 365–389. A similar theme, with different politics, may be found in Vilmos Holczhauser, *Konsens und Konflikt: Die Begriffe des Politischen bei Carl Schmitt* (Berlin: Duncker & Humblot, 1989).

[33] A fact also noted by Ellen Kennedy, in *Telos* 73, p. 66; and by Steven Lukes (in critique of Habermas), "Of Gods and Demons," in David Held and John B. Thompson, *Habermas: Critical Debates* (London: Macmillan, 1982), also cited by Kennedy.

no matter what else he might be, was not a democrat. He did not conceive sovereignty as something each individual might have but rather as the exercise of power by the state. It is to this central and "tough" notion of sovereignty that conservatives respond. The question raised here is whether one can accept the formulations of *The Concept of the Political* as (in Schmitt's words) "the starting point for objective discussion" and not emerge from them in the direction that Leo Strauss took.[34] I leave unanswered and barely asked if there could be a Straussianism of the Left in America, an alliance of Berkeley and Chicago, as it were.[35]

Legitimation and Enemies

In *The Concept of the Political*, Schmitt identifies as the "high points of politics" those moments in which "the enemy is, in concrete clarity, recognized as the enemy." He suggests that this is true both theoretically and in practice.[36] There are two aspects of this claim worthy of note. The first is the semi-Hegelian form it assumes. The concrete recognition of the other as enemy and the consequent establishment of one's own identity sounds something like Hegel's Master and Slave, especially if read through a Kojèvian lens. I suspect, in fact, that it is this aspect which led the SS journal *Das Schwarze Korps* to accuse Schmitt of neo-Hegelianism.[37]

But only the form is Hegelian. There are two elements in Schmitt's claim about enemies which are not Hegelian. First is a suggestion that unless one is clear about the fundamental nonratio-

[34] For some preliminary ideas see Gourevitch and Roth, "Introduction," to Leo Strauss, *On Tyranny,* as well as the material from Strauss and Kojève in that book.

[35] I find that Holmes, *Anatomy of Antiliberalism,* p. 88, raises and dismisses the question about Alasdair MacIntyre.

[36] CP 67. See the discussion in Meier, *Carl Schmitt and Leo Strauss,* pp. 28 ff.

[37] See Gottfried, *Carl Schmitt,* p. 31; Bendersky, *Carl Schmitt,* pp. 240 ff.

nality of politics, one will likely be overtaken by events. Following the passage about the "high points of politics," Schmitt goes on to give examples of those who were clear about what was friend and enemy and those who were not. He cites as clear-headed some German opponents of Napoleon; Lenin in his condemnation of capitalism; and—most strikingly—Cromwell in his enmity toward Spain. He contrasts these men to "the doomed classes [who] romanticized the Russian peasant," and to the "aristocratic society in France before the Revolution of 1789 [who] sentimentalized 'man who is by nature good.' "[38] The implication here is that rationality—what is rational for a group to do to preserve itself as a group—is not only not universal but hard to know. We are not far here from Alasdair MacIntyre's *Whose Justice? Whose Rationality?*[39] The important aspect to Schmitt's claim is that it is by facing the friend-enemy distinction that we (a "we") will be able to be clear about what "we" are and what it is "rational" for "us" to do.

Schmitt insists in his discussion of the friend-enemy distinction on the public nature of the categories. It is not my enemy but *our* enemy; that is, "enemy" is a political concept. Here Schmitt enlists the public quality to politics in order to prevent a universalism which he thinks extremely dangerous. The argument goes like this. Resistance to or the refusal to accept the fact that one's rational action has limitations determined by the quality of the identity of one's group leads to two possible outcomes.

The first is that one assumes one shares with others universal qualities which must then "naturally" engender an ultimate convergence of interests attainable through negotiation and compro-

---

[38] CP 68. See Bellamy and Baehr, *European Journal of Political Research* 23, pp. 180 ff.

[39] See Alasdair MacIntyre, *Whose Justice? Whose Rationality?* (Notre Dame: University of Notre Dame Press, 1988). Holmes, *Anatomy of Antiliberalism*, p. 88, draws attention to this possible link.

mise. Here events are most likely not only to prove one wrong but to destroy a group that acts on such a false belief. (One thinks of Marx's caustic comments about the social-democrats in *The Eighteenth Brumaire of Louis Napoleon*). This is the case with the "doomed" Russian classes and the "aristocratic society" of France.

The other, more dangerous possibility is that one will claim to speak in the name of universal humanity. In such a case, all those by whom one is opposed must perforce be seen as speaking against humanity and hence can only merit to be exterminated. Schmitt writes:

> Humanity as such and as a whole has no enemies. Everyone belongs to humanity . . . "Humanity" thus becomes an asymmetrical counter-concept. If he discriminates within humanity and thereby denies the quality of being human to a disturber or destroyer, then the negatively valued person becomes an unperson, and his life is no longer of the highest value: it becomes worthless and must be destroyed. Concepts such as "human being" thus contain the possibility of the deepest inequality and become thereby "asymmetrical."[40]

These words were written in 1976, but they were prepared for in the conclusion to *The Concept of the Political:* "The adversary is thus no longer called an enemy but a disturber of peace and is thereby designated to be an outlaw of humanity."[41] Schmitt wants here to remove from politics, especially international politics but also internal politics of an ideological kind, any possibility of justifying one's action on the basis of a claim to universal moral principles. He does so because he fears that in such a framework *all* claims to good will recognize no limits to their reach. And, thus, this century will see "wars for the domination of the earth" (the phrase is Nietzsche's in *Ecce Homo*), that is, wars to determine

---

[40] Carl Schmitt, "The Legal World Revolution," *Telos* 72 (Summer 1987), p. 88.

[41] CP 79; cf CP 54 ff.

once and for all what is good for all, wars with no outcome except an end to politics and the elimination of all difference.

On a first level, the question that Schmitt poses here is whether liberalism can meet the challenges posed by international politics.[42] Rousseau suggested that a country would be better off avoiding international politics; Hobbes made no attempt to extend the notion of sovereignty beyond state borders. Any answer to this question must deal with the fact that this century has seen not only the dramatic extension of countries claiming to adhere to universal values but also unprecedented attempts at local and universal genocide and the development of extremely aggressive regionalisms. For Schmitt these all went together. He thought there was no natural limit to what one might do to make the world safe for liberalism. The evidence is mixed.

On a second level, one must ask how a man who wrote with some eloquence about the dangers of universalism could have written what he wrote in support of Nazi policies. Three possible answers present themselves. The first is that he was morally blinded by ambition—that he would say what was necessary to attain and remain in prestigious posts. The second is that he did not understand what the Nazis were doing. The last is that he thought (or persuaded himself for some period of time) that the opponents of the regime were, in fact, enemies, who, in fact, posed a threat to the German identity. If the last is true, as I believe it to be, then what needs attention in Schmitt's theory is not the

---

[42] Questions also raised by scholars like Hans Morgenthau, whose early work in Germany focused on the *political* (and not legal) quality of international relations; and Henry Kissinger, whose *The Necessity for Choice* (New York: Harper, 1961) and "The White Revolutionary: Reflections on Bismarck," *Daedalus* 97, no. 3 (Summer 1968), pp. 888–924, while not mentioning Schmitt, clearly draw on him, as did some of Kissinger's practice as a statesman. Note the parallel title in Wolin's article, "Carl Schmitt, the Conservative Revolutionary." See Alfons Söllner, "German Conservativism in America: Morgenthau's Political Realism," *Telos* 72 (Summer 1987), pp. 161–172.

attack on universalism but the overly simplistic notion of friend. There is a way in which Schmitt allowed his notion of enemy to generate his idea of friend.

Schmitt and Nazism

Does one's judgment on Schmitt come down to the way one reads the facts of Schmitt's adherence to the Nazi Party? Among his more sympathetic commentators there is a tendency to apologize and excuse. At least one response given by those who sympathize with Schmitt's work will not do. This is the one repeated by the editors of *Telos* to Professor Jeffrey Herf: they rehearse answers like that of Paul Tillich, who responded to a student who objected to Heidegger on the grounds of his participation in the Nazi party by pointing out that Plato had after all served the tyrant Dionysos of Syracuse and we do not therefore refrain from reading him.[43] While the quality of a person's thought can in no way be reduced to a person's actions, this is only because no action admits, in a moment, of only the meaning that time will give to it. One cannot simply draw a line between thought and life as if choices in life could be judged by criteria foreign to thought. Context matters, and not in a self-evident way.[44] However, to ask the question of what Schmitt thought he was doing—his intentions— can also not be final. To understand everything is precisely *not* to excuse it. Purity of intentions matters for little and is often dangerous in politics.[45]

[43] *Telos* 74 (Winter 1987–88), p. 140.

[44] For a revelatory discussion of this matter in relation to the case of Heidegger's silences on himself, see Babette Babich, "The Ethical Alpha and the Linguistic Omega: Heidegger's Anti-Semitism and the Inner Affinity between Germany and Greece," *Joyful Wisdom: A Journal for Postmodern Ethics* 1, no. 1 (1994), pp. 3–25.

[45] This was the point of Max Weber's essay "Politics as a Vocation." See Hannah Arendt, *Eichmann in Jerusalem* (New York: Viking, 1964), Epilogue.

It seems to me relatively clear that in most aspects of his thought Schmitt's understanding of law and the world did not change throughout his life. This includes at least some aspects of his open anti-Semitism during the period 1933–36.[46] Frightening in Schmitt's case is the possibility that precisely what many find attractive in Schmitt must, while not requiring them to, open the possibility of the route he took. I want briefly to suggest that this is a question we must face. Consider the possibilities.

The approach taken by Strauss and Meier consists in arguing that Schmitt, while attempting a radical critique of liberalism, remains within the liberal framework. (Such an accusation is similar to the one Heidegger makes about Nietzsche as attempting a radical critique of Western metaphysics while remaining in the metaphysical framework.) The implication therefore is that the choices Schmitt makes are not excluded by the liberal framework; that is, they take place in the terms allowed by that framework. The question here becomes the manner in which one can mitigate the dangerous possibilities inherent in liberalism, since for the historical present and apparent future no alternative is available. The commitment to liberalism is thus instrumental.

The position taken by the contributors to *Telos* as well as many of Schmitt's other English-language defenders derives from the feeling that the liberal tradition no longer offers the intellectual resources to meet the challenges (especially those of technological domination and bureaucratized capitalism) of the modern world. Central to this pressing need for new theoretical resources is the

---

[46] See Nicolaus Sombart, *Die deutschen Männer und ihre Feinde: Carl Schmitt, ein deutsches Schicksal zwischen Männerbund und Matriarchatsmythos* (Munich: Hanser Verlag, 1991). I owe this reference to Holmes, *Anatomy of Antiliberalism,* and I share his anxiety about the psychoanalytic elements of Sombart's book as practiced on Schmitt. The most searching discussion of Schmitt's anti-Semitic writings and activities is Jacob Taubes, *Ad Carl Schmitt: Gegenstrebige Fügung* (Berlin: Merve Verlag, 1987). Taubes calls Schmitt "an apocalyptic of the Counterrevolution" (p. 7).

collapse of Marxism as a viable first-world theoretical stance. In this perspective, the preservation of (and, indeed, emphasis on) the forms of liberal institutions further undermines the values those institutions were originally supposed to promote. (This was the gist of Schmitt's analysis also, of course.) Here the rejection of liberal structures is made in the name of (more or less) liberal values. But the only structure proposed is a kinder and gentler antagonistics than the existentially intense ones in Schmitt.

Liberals are horrified at Schmitt because he offends against one of the deepest premises of liberalism: politics is necessary but should not become serious. As Robert Lane wrote a long time ago, liberal politics requires "a touch of anomie" about the public sphere.[47] Most important, liberal politics take the form of claiming that politics should never be about identity and that to the degree that policy decisions affect what it means to be a person those decisions are divisive and dangerous. For liberals, rights are rights no matter how gained: they have little truck with the claim of what one might call Schmitt-leaning democrats that rights are not rights unless they are fought for and won, such that they become *our* rights.[48]

Why these reactions now? There is no question but that the Left and the Right are, in their interest in Schmitt, responding to a perceived need to find other sources for political theorizing.[49] Clearly there is a sense that the political categories imposed on us

---

[47] Robert Lane, *Political Ideology* (Glencoe, IL: Free Press, 1962), p. 249. I believe I owe this reference and my first epigraph to my ancient friendship with Bruce Payne.

[48] See Sheldon S. Wolin, Review of John Rawls, *Political Liberalism,* forthcoming in *Political Theory* 24, no. 1 (February 1996).

[49] *Telos* continues to look to the right. The Summer 1994 issue is devoted to the writings of Alain de Benoist, a leading theoretician of the New French Right. The progressive Left (Benjamin Barber, Charles Taylor) finds sustenance in de Maistre and Herder. The Right becomes ever more Nietzschean in its condemnation of liberal society.

by the relation to the monarchy of various parts of the 1791 French National Assembly have played their way out in the face of modern technologically and rationalized industrial society.

There is also another reason, this one more generational. An intellectual consequence of the experience with Nazism was to effectively shrink, perhaps one might say homogenize, the language and terms of political debate in the subsequent period. As the Nazi experience fades from consciousness (at just over fifty years of age, I am among the last to have been born during the war and to have been taught by those with adult consciousness during the war), so also possibilities excluded by the specter of Auschwitz have returned. The revival of interest in Schmitt is consequent, I believe, to this increasing distance from the 1930s. How we manage the intellectual terrain that we are opening up is our responsibility.

TRANSLATOR'S NOTE
TO THE 1996 EDITION

For this edition, the translation of Leo Strauss's "Anmer-kungen zu Carl Schmitt, *Der Begriff des Politischen*" has been re-printed from Heinrich Meier, *Carl Schmitt and Leo Strauss: The Hidden Dialogue,* translated by J. Harvey Lomax (Chicago: Univer-sity of Chicago Press, 1995). My own Introduction to and transla-tion of Schmitt's essay are reprinted with minor corrections from Carl Schmitt, *The Concept of the Political* (New Brunswick, NJ: Rutgers University Press, 1976). Note 9 on page 6 refers to an earlier English version of the Strauss piece, not reproduced here. On page 10, line 17, on page 11, lines 2 and 3, and on page 14, line 3, I have inserted "militant" before "ideology" (pages 10 and 11) and before "political" (page 14) in order to better distinguish militant forms of ideology from secular forms.

George Schwab

ACKNOWLEDGMENTS

In the process of translating this essay I was fortunate in having been able to consult Professor Schmitt at his home in West Germany. His fascination for the English language resulted in many hours of fruitful discussions on the meaning of words. In preparing this translation for publication I am grateful to my friend and colleague, Mr. Frank D. Grande, for his suggestions and comments and also to Mrs. Erna Hilfstein for the time which she has put at my disposal in aiding me with some technical details. Of course, the sole responsibility for the translation rests upon the translator. For the grant advanced to complete this project I express my gratitude to the Research Foundation of The City University of New York.

George Schwab

The City College and
The City University of New York
July 1975

THE CONCEPT OF THE POLITICAL

by CARL SCHMITT

INTRODUCTION

I

The French political philosopher Julien Freund has observed that "by a curious paradox the name Schmitt is surrounded by mist, and it may be asked whether this fog is not often manufactured artificially. . . . It is fashionable to discredit the work of this author on the basis of a reputation that is based largely on rumors . . . [and] it is better . . . to recognize that Carl Schmitt is controversial and will always remain controversial, like all those who belong to the same intellectual family: Machiavelli, Hobbes, de Maistre, Donoso Cortés, and also Max Weber. . . ." [1]

No one indeed has questioned the prolificness of Schmitt, and few have questioned the profundity of his writings. But his decision, after the Enabling Act of March 1933, to become the self-appointed ideologue of the Nazis has made him so controversial [2] that even today it is difficult to view his work objectively. [3] The

[1] Preface to Francis Rosenstiel's *Le Principe de supranationalité: Essai sur les rapports de la politique et du droit* (Paris: Editions A. Pedone, 1962), pp. 15–16.

[2] See George Schwab, "Carl Schmitt: Political Opportunist?" *Intellect*, Vol. 103, No. 2363 (February, 1975), pp. 334–337; also, George Schwab, *The Challenge of the Exception: An Introduction to the Political Ideas of Carl Schmitt between 1921 and 1936* (Berlin: Duncker & Humblot, 1970), pp. 138–141, 149–150; Helmut Heiber, *Walter Frank und sein Reichsinstitut für Geschichte des neuen Deutschlands* (Stuttgart: Deutsche Verlags-Anstalt, 1966), p. 912.

[3] The animus against Schmitt is so great that in some circles it is fashionable to omit his name even in scholarly publications, as though Schmitt

3

problem of assessing Schmitt's writings has been further complicated for English-speaking students because none of his works has previously been translated into English.[4]

Carl Schmitt was born in 1888 into a family of devout Catholics in the predominantly Protestant town of Plettenberg in Westphalia. He received his initial formal education in a Catholic school. Later, while continuing his humanistic studies, he resided in a Catholic institution. Subsequently he studied law at the universities of Berlin and Strasbourg and received his doctorate in jurisprudence in 1910. After working as a law clerk, he entered the academic world and taught at the University of Strasbourg in 1916, at the Graduate School of Business Administration at Munich from 1919 to 1921, the universities of Greifswald in 1921, Bonn from 1922 to 1928, the Graduate School of Business Administration at Berlin from 1928 to 1933, and the universities of Cologne in 1933 and Berlin from 1933 to 1945.[5]

Schmitt's early writings reflect his consciousness of the *Kulturkampf* controversy which had occurred just prior to his birth. He

had never existed. For example, as Dr. Hans-Dietrich Sander has pointed out (*Marxistische Ideologie und allgemeine Kunsttheorie*, 2nd ed. (Tübingen: J. C. B. Mohr [Paul Siebeck], 1975), p. 173, it is part of the "intellectual civil war of our time" that the footnotes in which Walter Benjamin acknowledged Schmitt's influence on his *Ursprung des deutschen Trauerspiels* were omitted by the editors, Theodor W. Adorno and Gretel Adorno, in their two-volume edition of Benjamin's work, published in Frankfort on the Main in 1955. For almost complete listings of Schmitt's works see Piet Tommissen, "Carl Schmitt Bibliographie," *Festschrift für Carl Schmitt zum 70. Geburtstag,* ed. H. Barion, E. Forsthoff, W. Weber (Berlin: Duncker & Humblot, 1959), pp. 275–297, 303–304; also, Piet Tommissen, "Ergänzungsliste zur Carl Schmitt Bibliographie vom Jahre 1959," *Epirrhosis: Festgabe für Carl Schmitt,* ed. H. Barion, E.-W. Böckenförde, E. Forsthoff, W. Weber (Berlin: Duncker & Humblot, 1968), II, 742–748.

[4] Some of Schmitt's writings are already available in French, Italian, Japanese and Spanish.

[5] For a detailed biographical sketch of Schmitt see Schwab, *The Challenge,* pp. 13–18.

was fascinated by and proud of the power the Catholic Church had exerted on so powerful a figure as Bismarck. This pride can be seen in his early conception of the state as an entity whose function is to realize right (*Recht*). And because of the universal nature of the Catholic Church it was, according to Schmitt, in a better position to decide on what constitutes right than the many states then in existence.[6]

But World War I, Germany's defeat, and the controversial terms of the Versailles treaty produced a new political reality in Germany. This induced Schmitt to focus his attention on some of the concrete problems facing the Weimar republic.[7]

II

Outraged at the treatment accorded to Germany by the victors, Schmitt, in his answers to concrete legal questions, explored some of the political implications of the new reality. But in *The Concept of the Political* [8] in particular—undoubtedly one of the most important tracts of political thought of the twentieth century—he raises the discussion to a level which transcends Weimar Germany in both space and time.

In 1932, the late Leo Strauss commented on *The Concept of the Political,* and his comments are reproduced at the end of this

---

[6] Carl Schmitt, *Der Wert des Staates und die Bedeutung des Einzelnen* (Tübingen: J. C. B. Mohr [Paul Siebeck], 1914), pp. 2, 45–46, 95.

[7] For a discussion of Schmitt's intellectual heritage and also for his shift of attention see Schwab, *The Challenge,* pp. 18–28; also, Schwab, "Carl Schmitt: Political Opportunist?" pp. 334–335.

[8] The thesis of this didactic essay appeared originally in 1927 under the title "Der Begriff des Politischen" in *Archiv für Sozialwissenschaft und Sozialpolitik,* Vol. 58, No. 1, pp. 1–33. This essay was further elaborated and published in 1932 under the same title by Duncker & Humblot, Munich. This translation is based on the text of the 1932 edition, and for the sake of brevity omits Schmitt's foreword, three corollaries, and references which he added to the 1963 edition.

volume.[9] Here, however, I should like to point out that Schmitt raised the question: what is the modern European state? In his answer he attempted, on the one hand, to derive a model of this state, and, on the other, to focus particular attention on the centrifugal forces within the state that were responsible for tearing it apart. Though this essay contains only germs of what subsequently matured into a relatively complete model,[10] in the opening sentence of the 1932 essay Schmitt indivisibly linked state and politics. Reflecting on the connection between the two, he recently commented:

The decisive question . . . concerns the relationship of . . . state and politics. A doctrine which began to take shape in the sixteenth and seventeenth centuries, a doctrine inaugurated by Machiavelli, Jean Bodin, and Thomas Hobbes, endowed the state with an important monopoly: the European state became the sole subject of politics. Both state and politics were linked just as indivisibly as *polis* and politics in Aristotle.[11]

Concretely speaking, only states, and not just any domestic or international association, are the bearers of politics. Hence only states may conduct with each other relations which in an ultimate

[9] "Anmerkungen zu Carl Schmitt, Der Begriff des Politischen," *Archiv für Sozialwissenschaft und Sozialpolitik,* Vol. 67, No. 6, pp. 732–749. The English translation appeared in 1965 in Leo Strauss's *Spinoza's Critique of Religion,* tr. E. M. Sinclair (New York: Schocken Books), pp. 331–351. The discrepancies between my translation of Schmitt and the words and phrases in Strauss's comments are in most instances stylistic. However, when Sinclair translated the German word *Feind* with "foe," it appears that Strauss was not aware of the conceptual distinction inherent in the words "enemy" and "foe." See below, pp. 9–11.

[10] See in particular Carl Schmitt's *Der Nomos der Erde im Völkerrecht des Jus Publicum Europaeum,* 2nd ed. (Berlin: Duncker & Humblot, 1974).

[11] Carl Schmitt, *Le categorie del 'politico,'* ed. Gianfranco Miglio and Pierangelo Schiera (Bologna: Società editrice il Mulino, 1972), pp. 23–24. Although the German version of this preface has not been printed, Schmitt gave me a copy of the German typescript, from which this English version was prepared.

sense are binding on their respective members. Though such relations revolve fundamentally around questions pertaining to politics, this by no means implies that other categories—economic, religious, cultural—do not also come into play. Yet, according to Schmitt in the essay translated here, even ostensibly nonpolitical categories have the potential of becoming political. Once a nonpolitical category acuminates in politics, only the state is then in the position to decide on its interests and undertake appropriate actions. It thus follows that in concrete circumstances it is the prerogative of the state to define the content and course of politics.

Precisely because of the uniqueness of events, Schmitt found it impossible to provide an exhaustive or even a general definition of politics, one that would always hold true.[12] By combining his belief in the uniqueness of events with his belief that man is basically dangerous, Schmitt advanced a simple criterion of politics in this essay which so far has proven to be constant, namely, the distinction between friend and enemy.

Although Schmitt is not one of those in Germany who consider war to be a social ideal, something to be cherished, or something normal, it is, nevertheless, an ever present possibility.[13] But the decision as to whether or not to go to war is a purely political decision and hence, in Schmitt's construction, something only the state can decide.[14] More precisely, as a state cannot exist without a

[12] On Schmitt's refusal to define politics, see the discussion by Julien Freund in his preface to the French translation of Schmitt's essay. *La Notion de politique* and *Théorie du partisan* (Paris: Calmann-Lévy, 1972), pp. 22–27.

[13] Of the numerous legends that surround Schmitt's ideas, Walter Laqueur in his otherwise interesting discussion of Weimar Germany echoes several, including the assertion that Schmitt's philosophy contained a "nihilist element" because it "justified war." *Weimar: A Cultural History 1918–1933* (New York: G. P. Putnam's Sons, 1974), p. 100.

[14] Because sovereign states constantly confront each other in the political arena with the obvious implication of the ever present possibility of war, the late Leo Strauss in his comments on Schmitt's essay, correctly observed that a connection exists between Schmitt and Thomas Hobbes. Whether one speaks

sovereign authority, it is this authority which in the final analysis
decides whether such an extreme situation is at hand.[15] Schmitt thus
links state, politics, and sovereignty.

This linking of state, politics, and sovereignty makes it clear
that Schmitt's major concern is with the modern sovereign state as
it began to emerge in the sixteenth and seventeenth centuries. From
the general tone of the essay it is also clear that he personally identified himself with this epoch and laments that the curtain was
descending. It may well be asked why he should object to the closing
of this period—especially in view of its violence. Although one can
extract the answer from his 1932 essay, he provided it himself in
some of his subsequent writings.

With exceptions, the epoch of the European sovereign state
may be characterized as a period in which order prevailed within
sovereign states and also in the relations between sovereign states.
The Peace of Augsburg (1555), the religious compromise of Eliza-
beth I (1559–1563), and the Edict of Nantes (1598) were significant

---

of the possibility of war or the conflict itself, one difference between Schmitt
and Hobbes is that, whereas for the latter it "is the state of war of individuals
—for Schmitt it is the state of war of groups, and especially of nations."
Though it is true that states in Schmitt's construction are constantly con-
fronted by this possibility, and from this view might be said to exist in a
state of nature, a qualitative difference does exist between Hobbes's and
Schmitt's state of nature [see Helmut Rumpf, *Carl Schmitt und Thomas
Hobbes: Ideelle Beziehungen und aktuelle Bedeutung mit einer Abhandlung
über die Frühschriften Carl Schmitts* (Berlin: Duncker & Humblot, 1972),
pp. 78–86]. Precisely because certain explicit conventions governed relations
of sovereign states in time of war, thereby overcoming the foe concept (see
pp. 9–11 below), we are not justified in ascribing to Schmitt a sort of
Hobbesian state of nature. At the critical point in Hobbes's state of nature
man may truly find himself in actual combat, and in such a situation, according to Hobbes, "nothing can be Unjust. The notions of Right and Wrong,
Justice and Injustice have there no place. . . . Force and Fraud, are in warre
the two Cardinall vertues" (*Leviathan,* Chap. 13).

[15] See Carl Schmitt, *Politische Theologie: Vier Kapitel zur Lehre von
der Souveränität* (Munich: Duncker & Humblot, 1922, 1934), p. 11.

steps in the movement toward religious toleration—the recognition on the part of newly emerging sovereign rulers in distinct territorial states [16] that Christians, regardless of specific doctrinal differences, were entitled to be treated as Christians and not as beings possessed by the devil to whom no quarter should be given. Once it was accepted in principle that Christians are equal by virtue of belonging to the same religion, developments at home had definite repercussions insofar as relations among sovereign states were concerned.

Hence, despite doctrinal differences, Catholic and Protestant rulers were prepared to coexist in a larger community. An implication of this development was that agreements could be concluded by sovereign states in time of peace with a reasonable expectation that these would be adhered to. Moreover, a secularized notion of politics enabled rules and regulations to emerge which applied in time of war as well. And this mitigated the devastation that had characterized past conflicts.[17]

Among other things, the emerging *jus publicum Europaeum* clearly distinguished a state of peace from that of war, and clear-cut distinctions were also drawn between combatants and noncombatants, between combat and noncombat areas, and the cessation of hostilities was usually followed by a peace treaty. Furthermore, prisoners of war were entitled to be treated humanely, and the concept of neutrality was also sanctioned.[18]

These developments contributed to changing the concept of the public adversary, something Schmitt did not see very clearly in

[16] Despite nominally reasserting the traditional allegiance owed by princes to the emperor, empire, and diet, the treaty of Westphalia (1648) stipulated that princes in their respective territorial domains were sovereign "in matters both ecclesiastical and political" (Article 64). Article 65 considerably reinforced the previous one by ascribing to the princes their right of "making or interpreting laws and declaring wars. . . ."

[17] See, for example, Lynn Montross, *War Through the Ages,* 3rd ed. (New York: Harper & Brothers, 1960), pp. 338–339, 385, 392, 394, 400.

[18] See Schmitt, *Der Nomos,* pp. 97–100, 112–143; also Schmitt's *Ex Captivitate Salus* (Köln: Greven Verlag, 1950), pp. 56–58.

1932.[19] What we in fact witness is the transformation of the foe concept in favor of the public enemy notion, i.e., the subjection of warfare to prescribed rules and regulations; hence feelings of personal hatred—so rampant when ideology dominates politics—subsided.[20] Schmitt alluded to this in 1932 when he said in the essay translated here that the enemy no longer had to be "hated personally" and that an "enemy exists only when, at least potentially, one fighting collectivity of people confronts a similar collectivity." The secularization of politics thus facilitated the growth of the *jus publicum Europaeum*, and this was accompanied by a new mode of warfare in which the adversary was considered a "clean" enemy. In 1963 Schmitt observed that the secularization of politics constituted a definite mark of "progress in the sense of humanity." [21]

Despite critical attacks on the sovereign state and the *jus publicum Europaeum* that accompanied its development (e.g., the French revolution and the Napoleonic wars, and, in the domain of political thought, the infusion of militant ideology into politics by Marx and Engels), the state withstood these until the early part of the twentieth century. But the rapid succession of momentous events—World War I, Versailles, the Communist victory in Moscow, and the Nazi victory in Berlin about one year after the publication of the 1932 text of Schmitt's essay—halted the broad course of development of the epoch of the European sovereign state and also soon showed that the traditional European sovereign state was no longer a politically viable entity in a rapidly changing world.

[19] See Schmitt's foreword to the 1963 edition of *Der Begriff des Politischen* (Berlin: Duncker & Humblot), pp. 17–19.

[20] The conceptual distinction inherent in the words "enemy" and "foe," and some of the implications of this distinction are treated by George Schwab in "Enemy oder Foe: Der Konflikt der modernen Politik," tr. J. Zeumer, *Epirrhosis*, II, 665–682. See also George Schwab, *The Challenge*, pp. 53–55; Ion X. Contiades, " 'ΕΧΘΡΟΣ' und 'ΠΟΛΕΜΙΟΣ' in der modernen politischen Theorie und der griechischen Antike," *Griechische Humanistische Gesellschaft*, Zweite Reihe (Athens, 1969), pp. 5 ff.

[21] See Schmitt's foreword to the 1963 edition of *Der Begriff*, p. 11.

Moreover, as this state rested on and functioned under a secular notion of politics, the infusion of militant ideology into politics undermined the state's very foundation. By virtue of its contamination with militant ideology, the new politics possessed a sort of "surplus value."[22] Thus the ideologically committed totalitarian one-party states readily dismissed the principle on which the *jus publicum Europaeum* was predicated, namely, the genuine acceptance by sovereign states of the principle *pacta sunt servanda.* The rules of the game governing relations of sovereign states were, therefore, no longer sacrosanct but were incorporated into the arsenal of weapons of one-party states and utilized as tactical devices in gaining specific ends. And, finally, with the victory of ideologies considered to be a true and absolute one, the adversary was no longer considered a "clean" enemy, but a despised foe to whom no quarter should be given.

III

Though Schmitt clearly saw in 1932 that the curtain was descending on an epoch, he undoubtedly would have welcomed the arrest and even the reversal of this process. It may perhaps be argued that, in view of Germany's central geographic location in Europe, its resources, level of industrialization, and overall potential, a politically healthy Germany could have aided in halting this process, at least temporarily. Yet, despite Germany's assets, she was unable to reassert herself in the arena of world politics, not because of policies pursued by her former adversaries, but primarily because of domestic economic and political circumstances. Since she was unable to put her house in order, Schmitt in 1932 continued rather despairingly to point to what he thought to be sensible solutions to halt the disintegration of the Weimar state.

[22] In a related context, I have discussed this question in "Appeasement and Detente: Some Reflections," *Detente in Historical Perspective,* ed. George Schwab and Henry Friedlander (New York: Cyrco Press, 1975), p. 140.

Thus, in "The Concept of the Political" and in many of his other writings, Schmitt focused attention on the immediate centrifugal forces tearing the Weimar state apart and on some of the intellectual underpinnings of these forces, including pluralism. As is well known, the theory of pluralism maintains that an individual is a member of many rather than just one human association, and no association, including the state, is necessarily the decisive and sovereign one. In the competition among associations for the loyalty of individuals, the individual is left to decide for himself the extent to which he may desire to become involved. Precisely such a doctrine, according to Schmitt, helps to undermine the state as the highest and most decisive entity.

Though formulated as a theory only recently, some of the concrete manifestations were already somewhat more than faintly visible in the sixteenth and seventeenth centuries. It was of particular concern to Schmitt that certain political forces which emerged in the modern state had begun to question and even challenge the state's monopoly on politics. The appearance and growth of such domestic forces often caused states to immerse themselves in internal political struggles, and this not only weakened the state's posture vis-à-vis other states, but undermined the sovereign state in general.

In other words, as long as the state's monopoly on politics was not seriously challenged from within, its posture, depending of course on the state's overall resources, was one of strength. The state's immersion in domestic political struggles and some of the consequences of this underlies Schmitt's discussion. In reflecting on this added dimension Schmitt was led to draw a distinction between "politics" and "political." His decision not to entitle his essay *The Concept of Politics* but, instead, *The Concept of the Political*, is a reflection of this distinction.

Whereas state and politics were indivisibly linked in the classical European state, Schmitt recently observed that

the classical profile of the state was shattered as its monopoly on politics waned. New . . . political protagonists asserted themselves. . . . From this followed a new degree of reflection for theoretical thought. Now one could distinguish "politics" from "political." The new protagonists become the core of the entire complex of problems called "political." Here lies the beginning and thrust of every attempt to recognize the many new subjects of the political, which become active in political reality, in the politics of the state or nonstate, and which bring about new kinds of friend-enemy groupings.[23]

Bearing in mind the circumstances under which Weimar was born, the liberal democratic nature of its constitution, and the extremist political movements which were permitted to thrive there, Schmitt, as already observed, was appalled at how the state was being turned into a whipping post, and his hope was to turn the situation around.

In his endeavor to strengthen the Weimar state, Schmitt challenged a basic liberal assumption then widely held either for philosophical or tactical reasons, namely, that every political party, no matter how antirepublican, must be permitted freely to compete for parliamentary representation and for governmental power.[24] This meant that the sole requirement of such parties in their quest for power was that they proceed legally.[25] Because the most influential commentators and jurists of the Weimar constitution argued that it was an open document insofar as any and all constitutional revisions are permissible if these are brought about legally,[26] a totalitarian

[23] Schmitt, *Le categorie*, p. 24. The English version was prepared from a copy of the German typescript.

[24] Cognizant of what had happened in Weimar, the Basic Law of Bonn permits the outlawing of negative political parties (Article 21).

[25] See Gotthard Jasper, *Der Schutz der Republik: Studien zur staatlichen Sicherung der Demokratie in der Weimarer Republik 1922–1930* (Tübingen: J. C. B. Mohr [Paul Siebeck], 1963), pp. 11, 14–15.

[26] Richard Thoma, a leading jurist, stated that the Reich's legislature "possesses an unlimited competence, a *plenitudo potestatis* for constitutional change" in "Die Funktionen der Staatsgewalt," *Handbuch des Deutschen Staatsrechts*, ed. G. Anschütz and R. Thoma (Tübingen: J. C. B. Mohr [Paul Siebeck], 1932), II, 154. Gerhard Anschütz, one of the leading commentators, noted that "the constitution does not stand above the legislature, but is at its

movement which succeeds in legally capturing the legislature can then proceed legally to forge a constitution and state that would reflect its militant political ideology.

Cognizant that the political left and right utilized bourgeois legality as a weapon in the quest for power and fearful of a victory by one of the extremist movements with the ideological subversion of the state certain to follow, Schmitt saw little hope in the ability of the Weimar state to survive unless its leadership was immediately prepared to distinguish friend from enemy and to act accordingly. Concretely speaking, he argued in 1932 that only those parties not intent on subverting the state be granted the right to compete for parliamentary and governmental power.[27] This obviously meant driving the extremists on both sides of the political spectrum from the open arena.[28]

Given the relative ease with which basic constitutional revisions could be brought about (Article 76), and the widespread adherence to legalist thinking—factors militating against the effectiveness of the presidency—Schmitt, toward the end of the Weimar period, sought to strengthen drastically the president's hands, and hence he developed the idea of a presidential system. Although his presidential system had its roots in the Weimar constitution, Schmitt's conception went beyond this document and was, there-

---

disposal" and that therefore there were no limits on the extent to which the constitution could be amended, including its abrogation (G. Anschütz, *Die Verfassung des Deutschen Reichs vom 11. August 1919,* 14th ed. [Berlin: Georg Stilke, 1933], pp. 401, 405). Because of the fate of the Weimar constitution, the Basic Law of Bonn recognizes sacrosanct parts (Article 79).

[27] Carl Schmitt, *Legalität und Legitimität* (Munich: Duncker & Humblot, 1932; Berlin, 1968), pp. 30–40.

[28] Heinrich Muth is correct in concluding that someone who advanced such a thought with great precision could under no circumstances have been in 1932 a member of the Nazi party nor a follower nor one who shared its ideas ("Carl Schmitt in der deutschen Innenpolitik des Sommers 1932," *Historische Zeitschrift, Beiheft* [1971], p. 97). This conclusion is particularly significant when one considers the erroneous insistence by some that Schmitt paved the way for the *Führerstaat.*

fore, no longer in accord with the constitution's spirit and letter. In other words, he was willing to sacrifice a part of the constitution in order to save and strengthen the existing state. By advocating such an extreme position, a position certainly unacceptable to the legalists, Schmitt clearly implied, among other things, that he would accept political parties and the Weimar parliament only on the condition that they be subordinate to and united with the president in the search for solutions.

As I have noted elsewhere, Schmitt's presidential system centered on the popularly elected president. As commander-in-chief of the armed forces, with the potent Article 48 of the Weimar constitution at his disposal and aided in his exercise of power by the bureaucracy and Reichswehr, the president, in Schmitt's view, could certainly have arrested the political assaults on the state.[29] Yet today it is widely charged that the presidential system which came about in the last years of Weimar had in fact paved the way for Hitler. But this misses Schmitt's point.

The system which finally emerged was an emasculated form of what he had urged. Hence, despite Schmitt's pleas for the necessity of distinguishing friend from enemy, Hindenburg consistently labored under the impact of legalist doctrines and did not, therefore, forcefully move to arrest and eliminate the political challenges facing Weimar. Quite the contrary. Not only did he continue to permit negatively inclined parties to operate and compete for power, but he also loathed ruling by decree.[30] It appears that he was under the confused impression that rule by decree might contradict the oath to defend the constitution which he took upon assuming the presidency (Article 42).[31]

[29] Schwab, *The Challenge,* pp. 80–89.

[30] See Hans Otto Meissner, Harry Wilde, *Die Machtergreifung: Ein Bericht über die Technik des Nationalsozialistischen Staatsstreichs* (Stuttgart: J. G. Cotta'sche Buchhandel, 1958), p. 119.

[31] According to Theodor Eschenburg, it had never occurred to Hindenburg to undertake extreme measures to save the constitution. "Die Rolle der Persönlichkeit in der Krise der Weimarer Verfassung: Hindenburg,

This impression is decisively reinforced by the letter Prelate Ludwig Kaas, head of the Center party, sent Chancellor Kurt von Schleicher on January 26, 1933.[32] A copy was also forwarded to Hindenburg.[33] The gist of the letter was that, since Chancellor Schleicher possessed no parliamentary backing, he should be dismissed and his place immediately assumed by Hitler, who not only controlled the largest party in the Reichstag but also promised to find a working majority by calling for new elections. In other words, Kaas's letter clearly implied that Hitler's appointment and new elections would assure a return to regular constitutional procedures, and Kaas insisted that it was absolutely incumbent upon Schleicher and Hindenburg not to follow the unconstitutional doctrines of Carl Schmitt and his followers,[34] namely, among other things, the infusion of the friend-enemy criterion into domestic political struggles. Kaas's letter explains Hindenburg's *volte face* vis-à-vis Hitler,[35] and Hitler's appointment confirmed Schmitt's forebodings for the Weimar state.

Brüning, Groener, Schleicher," *Vierteljahrshefte für Zeitgeschichte*, Heft 1 (January, 1961), p. 6.

[32] This letter was made public on January 29, 1933—one day before Hitler's appointment. Reprinted in *Jahrbuch des öffentlichen Rechts der Gegenwart*, 21 (1933/34), 141–142.

[33] *Die Protokolle der Reichstagsfraktion und des Fraktionsvorstands der deutschen Zentrumspartei, 1926–1933*, ed. Rudolf Morsey (Mainz: Matthias-Grünewald-Verlag, 1969), p. 609.

[34] *Jahrbuch*, p. 142. See also Schmitt's note on this crucial episode in his *Verfassungsrechtliche Aufsätze aus den Jahren 1924–1954* (Berlin: Duncker & Humblot, 1958, 1973), pp. 349–350.

[35] Although Andreas Dorpalen does not mention this letter, it is evident from his account of *Hindenburg and the Weimar Republic* (Princeton: Princeton University Press, 1964) that the President's *volte face* was quite sudden (pp. 431–432) and that he finally became convinced that Hitler's appointment "was the only constitutional solution . . ." (p. 433).

TRANSLATOR'S NOTE

As a rule Schmitt's style does not suffer from the usual problems one encounters in what is generally known as "professorial German." Nevertheless, it has at times proved difficult to translate his thoughts with clarity and precision. Wherever possible, therefore, the translator has divided long paragraphs and sentences and even shortened some of the latter, without impairing the ideas Schmitt conveys. Furthermore, a number of citations pertaining mainly to specific legal questions which have no relevance to the English reader were omitted. But a minimum of explanatory notes (marked by asterisks) has been added whenever the translator considered these important in helping the reader put the question discussed in proper perspective.

THE CONCEPT
OF THE POLITICAL

*In memory of my friend, August Schaetz of Munich, who
fell on August 28, 1917, in the assault on Moncelul*

I

The concept of the state presupposes the concept of the
political.

According to modern linguistic usage, the state is the political
status of an organized people in an enclosed territorial unit. This is
nothing more than a general paraphrase, not a definition of the
state. Since we are concerned here with the nature of the political,
such a definition is unwarranted. It may be left open what the state
is in its essence—a machine or an organism, a person or an institution, a society or a community, an enterprise or a beehive, or perhaps even a basic procedural order. These definitions and images
anticipate too much meaning, interpretation, illustration, and construction, and therefore cannot constitute any appropriate point of
departure for a simple and elementary statement.

In its literal sense and in its historical appearance the state is a
specific entity of a people.* Vis-à-vis the many conceivable kinds of

* Schmitt has in mind the modern national sovereign state and not the
political entities of the medieval or ancient periods. For Schmitt's identifica-
tion with the epoch of the modern state see George Schwab, *The Challenge
of the Exception: An Introduction to the political Ideas of Carl Schmitt between
1921 and 1936* 2d ed. (New York: Greenwood Press, 1989), pp. 27, 54; also,

entities, it is in the decisive case the ultimate authority. More need
not be said at this moment. All characteristics of this image of entity
and people receive their meaning from the further distinctive trait
of the political and become incomprehensible when the nature of
the political is misunderstood.

One seldom finds a clear definition of the political. The word
is most frequently used negatively, in contrast to various other ideas,
for example in such antitheses as politics and economy, politics and
morality, politics and law; and within law there is again politics
and civil law,[1] and so forth. By means of such negative, often also
polemical confrontations, it is usually possible, depending upon the
context and concrete situation, to characterize something with clarity. But this is still not a specific definition. In one way or another
"political" is generally juxtaposed to "state" or at least is brought
into relation with it.[2] The state thus appears as something political,
the political as something pertaining to the state—obviously an un-
satisfactory circle.

George Schwab, "Enemy oder Foe: Der Konflikt der modernen Politik,"
tr. J. Zeumer, *Epirrhosis: Festgabe für Carl Schmitt*, ed. H. Barion, E.-W.
Böckenförde, E. Forsthoff, W. Weber (Berlin: Duncker & Humblot, 1968),
II, 665–666.

[1] The antithesis of law and politics is easily confused by the antithesis
of civil and public law. According to J. K. Bluntschli in *Allgemeines Staatsrecht*, 4th ed. (Munich: J. G. Cotta, 1868), I, 219: "Property is a civil law and
not a political concept." The political significance of this antithesis came
particularly to the fore in 1925 and 1926, during the debates regarding the
expropriation of the fortunes of the princes who had formerly ruled in Germany. The following sentence from the speech by deputy Dietrich (Reichstag
session, December 2, 1925, *Berichte*, 4717) is cited as an example: "We are of
the opinion that the issues here do not at all pertain to civil law questions
but are purely political ones. . . ."

[2] Also in those definitions of the political which utilize the concept of
power as the decisive factor, this power appears mostly as state power, for
example, in Max Weber's "Politik als Beruf," *Gesammelte politische Schriften*, 3rd ed., ed. Johannes Winckelmann (Tübingen: J. C. B. Mohr [Paul
Siebeck], 1971), pp. 505, 506: "aspiring to participate in or of influencing
the distribution of power, be it between states, be it internally between groups

Many such descriptions of the political appear in professional juridic literature. Insofar as these are not politically polemical, they are of practical and technical interest and are to be understood as legal or administrative decisions in particular cases. These then receive their meaning by the presupposition of a stable state within whose framework they operate. Thus there exists, for example, a jurisprudence and literature pertaining to the concept of the political club or the political meeting in the law of associations. Furthermore, French administrative law practice has attempted to construct a concept of the political motive (*mobile politique*) with whose aid political acts of government (*actes de gouvernement*) could be distinguished from nonpolitical administrative acts and thereby removed from the control of administrative courts.[3]

Such accommodating definitions serve the needs of legal prac-

---

of people which the state encompasses," or "leadership or the influencing of a political association, hence today, of a state"; or his "Parliament und Regierung im neugeordneten Deutschland," *ibid.*, p. 347: "The essence of politics is . . . combat, the winning of allies and of voluntary followers." H. Triepel, *Staatsrecht und Politik* (Berlin: W. de Gruyter & Co., 1927), pp. 16–17, says: "Until recent decades politics was still plainly associated with the study of the state. . . . In this vein Weitz characterizes politics as the learned discussion of the state with respect to the historical development of states on the whole as well as of their current conditions and needs." Triepel then justly criticizes the ostensibly nonpolitical, purely juristic approach of the Gerber-Laband school and the attempt at its continuation in the postwar period (Kelsen). Nevertheless, Triepel had not yet recognized the pure political meaning of this pretense of an apolitical purity, because he subscribes to the equation politics = state. As will still be seen below, designating the adversary as political and oneself as nonpolitical (i.e., scientific, just, objective, neutral, etc.) is in actuality a typical and unusually intensive way of pursuing politics.

[3] . . . For the criterion of the political furnished here (friend-enemy orientation), I draw upon the particularly interesting definition of the specifically political *acte de gouvernement* which Dufour . . . (*Traité de droit administratif appliqué*, V, 128) has advanced: "Defining an act of government is the purpose to which the author addresses himself. Such an act aims at defending society itself or as embodied in the government against its internal or external enemies, overt or covert, present or future. . . ."

tice. Basically, they provide a practical way of delimiting legal competences of cases within a state in its legal procedures. They do not in the least aim at a general definition of the political. Such definitions of the political suffice, therefore, for as long as the state and the public institutions can be assumed as something self-evident and concrete. Also, the general definitions of the political which contain nothing more than additional references to the state are understandable and to that extent also intellectually justifiable for as long as the state is truly a clear and unequivocal eminent entity confronting nonpolitical groups and affairs—in other words, for as long as the state possesses the monopoly on politics. That was the case where the state had either (as in the eighteenth century) not recognized society as an antithetical force or, at least (as in Germany in the nineteenth century and into the twentieth), stood above society as a stable and distinct force.

The equation state = politics becomes erroneous and deceptive at exactly the moment when state and society penetrate each other. What had been up to that point affairs of state become thereby social matters, and, vice versa, what had been purely social matters become affairs of state—as must necessarily occur in a democratically organized unit. Heretofore ostensibly neutral domains—religion, culture, education, the economy—then cease to be neutral in the sense that they do not pertain to state and to politics. As a polemical concept against such neutralizations and depoliticalizations of important domains appears the total state, which potentially embraces every domain. This results in the identity of state and society. In such a state, therefore, everything is at least potentially political, and in referring to the state it is no longer possible to assert for it a specifically political characteristic.

[Schmitt's Note]

The development can be traced from the absolute state of the eighteenth century via the neutral (noninterventionist) state of the nineteenth to the total state of the twentieth.[4] Democracy must do away with all the typical distinctions and depoliticalizations characteristic of the liberal nineteenth century, also with those corresponding to the nineteenth-century antitheses and divisions pertaining to the state-society (= political against social) contrast, namely the following, among numerous other thoroughly polemical and thereby again political antitheses:

religious	as antithesis of political
cultural	as antithesis of political
economic	as antithesis of political
legal	as antithesis of political
scientific	as antithesis of political

The more profound thinkers of the nineteenth century soon recognized this. In Jacob Burckhardt's *Weltgeschichtliche Betrachtungen* (of the period around 1870) the following sentences are found on "democracy, i.e., a doctrine nourished by a thousand springs, and varying greatly with the social status of its adherents. Only in one respect was it consistent, namely, in the insatiability of its demand for state control of the individual. Thus it blurs the boundaries between state and society and looks to the state for the things that society will most likely refuse to do, while maintaining a permanent condition of argument and change and ultimately vindicating the right to work and subsistence for certain castes." Burckhardt also correctly noted the inner contradiction of democracy and the liberal constitutional state: "The state is thus, on the one hand, the realization and expression of the cultural ideas of every party; on the other, merely the visible vestures of civic life and powerful on an *ad hoc* basis only. It should be able to do everything, yet allowed to do nothing. In particular, it must not defend its existing form in any crisis—and after all, what men want more

[4] See Carl Schmitt, *Der Hüter der Verfassung* (Tübingen: J. C. B. Mohr [Paul Siebeck], 1931; Berlin: Duncker & Humblot, 1969), pp. 78–79.

than anything else is to participate in the exercise of its power. The state's form thus becomes increasingly questionable and its radius of power ever broader." [5]

German political science originally maintained (under the impact of Hegel's philosophy of the state) that the state is qualitatively distinct from society and higher than it. A state standing above society could be called universal but not total, as that term is understood nowadays, namely, as the polemical negation of the neutral state, whose economy and law were in themselves nonpolitical. Nevertheless, after 1848, the qualitative distinction between state and society to which Lorenz von Stein and Rudolf Gneist still subscribed lost its previous clarity. Notwithstanding certain limitations, reservations, and compromises, the development of German political science, whose fundamental lines are shown in my treatise on Preuss,[6] follows the historical development toward the democratic identity of state and society.

An interesting national-liberal intermediary stage is recognizable in the works of Albert Haenel. "To generalize the concept of state altogether with the concept of human society" is, according to him, a "downright mistake." He sees in the state an entity joining other organizations of society but of a "special kind which rises above these and is all embracing." Although its general purpose is universal, though only in the special task of delimiting and organizing socially effective forces, i.e., in the specific function of the law, Haenel considers wrong the belief that the state has, at least potentially, the power of making all the social goals of humanity its goals too. Even though the state is for him universal, it is by no means total.[7] The decisive step is found in Gierke's theory of association (the first volume of his *Das deutsche Genossenschaftsrecht* appeared

---

[5] Kröner's edition, pp. 133, 135, 197.

[6] *Hugo Preuss: Sein Staatsbegriff und seine Stellung in der deutschen Staatslehre* (Tübingen: J. C. B. Mohr [Paul Siebeck], 1930).

[7] *Studien zum Deutschen Staatsrechte* (Leipzig: Verlag von H. Haessel, 1888), II, 219; *Deutsches Staatsrecht* (Leipzig: Duncker & Humblot, 1892), I, 110.

in 1868), because it conceives of the state as one association equal to other associations. Of course, in addition to the associational elements, sovereign ones too belonged to the state and were sometimes stressed more and sometimes less. But, since it pertained to a theory of association and not to a theory of sovereignty of the state, the democratic consequences were undeniable. In Germany, they were drawn by Hugo Preuss and K. Wolzendorff, whereas in England it led to pluralist theories (see below, Section 4).

While awaiting further enlightenment, it seems to me that Rudolf Smend's theory of the integration of the state corresponds to a political situation in which society is no longer integrated into an existing state (as the German people in the monarchical state of the nineteenth century) but should itself integrate into the state. That this situation necessitates the total state is expressed most clearly in Smend's remark about a sentence from H. Trescher's 1918 dissertation on Montesquieu and Hegel.[8] There it is said of Hegel's doctrine of the division of powers that it signifies "the most vigorous penetration of all societal spheres by the state for the general purpose of winning for the entirety of the state all vital energies of the people." To which Smend adds that this is "precisely the integration theory" of his book. In actuality it is the total state which no longer knows anything absolutely nonpolitical, the state which must do away with the depoliticalizations of the nineteenth century and which in particular puts an end to the principle that the apolitical economy is independent of the state and that the state is apart from the economy.

-------- • --------

2

A definition of the political can be obtained only by discovering and defining the specifically political categories. In contrast to the various relatively independent endeavors of human thought and

[8] Rudolf Smend, *Verfassung und Verfassungsrecht* (Munich: Duncker & Humblot, 1928), p. 97, note 2.

action, particularly the moral, aesthetic, and economic, the political has its own criteria which express themselves in a characteristic way. The political must therefore rest on its own ultimate distinctions, to which all action with a specifically political meaning can be traced. Let us assume that in the realm of morality the final distinctions are between good and evil, in aesthetics beautiful and ugly, in economics profitable and unprofitable. The question then is whether there is also a special distinction which can serve as a simple criterion of the political and of what it consists. The nature of such a political distinction is surely different from that of those others. It is independent of them and as such can speak clearly for itself.

The specific political distinction to which political actions and motives can be reduced is that between friend and enemy.* This provides a definition in the sense of a criterion and not as an exhaustive definition or one indicative of substantial content.† Insofar as it is not derived from other criteria, the antithesis of friend and enemy corresponds to the relatively independent criteria of other antitheses: good and evil in the moral sphere, beautiful and ugly in the aesthetic sphere, and so on. In any event it is independent, not in the sense of a distinct new domain, but in that it can neither be based on any one antithesis or any combination of other antitheses, nor can it be traced to these. If the antithesis of good and evil is not simply identical with that of beautiful and ugly, profitable and unprofitable, and cannot be directly reduced to the others, then the antithesis of friend and enemy must even less be confused with or mistaken for the others. The distinction of friend and enemy denotes the utmost degree of intensity of a union or separation, of an association or dissociation. It can exist theo-

---

* Since Schmitt identified himself with the epoch of the national sovereign state with its *jus publicum Europaeum,* he used the term *Feind* in the enemy and not the foe sense.

† Of the numerous discussions of Schmitt's friend-enemy criterion, particular attention is called to Hans Morgenthau's *La Notion du "politique" et la théorie des différends internationaux* (Paris: Sirey, 1933), pp. 35–37, 44–64. The critique contained therein and Schmitt's influence on him is often implied in Morgenthau's subsequent writings.

retically and practically, without having simultaneously to draw upon all those moral, aesthetic, economic, or other distinctions. The political enemy need not be morally evil or aesthetically ugly; he need not appear as an economic competitor, and it may even be advantageous to engage with him in business transactions. But he is, nevertheless, the other, the stranger; and it is sufficient for his nature that he is, in a specially intense way, existentially something different and alien, so that in the extreme case conflicts with him are possible. These can neither be decided by a previously determined general norm nor by the judgment of a disinterested and therefore neutral third party.

Only the actual participants can correctly recognize, understand, and judge the concrete situation and settle the extreme case of conflict. Each participant is in a position to judge whether the adversary intends to negate his opponent's way of life and therefore must be repulsed or fought in order to preserve one's own form of existence. Emotionally the enemy is easily treated as being evil and ugly, because every distinction, most of all the political, as the strongest and most intense of the distinctions and categorizations, draws upon other distinctions for support. This does not alter the autonomy of such distinctions. Consequently, the reverse is also true: the morally evil, aesthetically ugly or economically damaging need not necessarily be the enemy; the morally good, aesthetically beautiful, and economically profitable need not necessarily become the friend in the specifically political sense of the word. Thereby the inherently objective nature and autonomy of the political becomes evident by virtue of its being able to treat, distinguish, and comprehend the friend-enemy antithesis independently of other antitheses.

3

The friend and enemy concepts are to be understood in their concrete and existential sense, not as metaphors or symbols, not mixed and weakened by economic, moral, and other conceptions, least of all in a private-individualistic sense as a psychological expression of private emotions and tendencies. They are neither normative nor pure spiritual antitheses. Liberalism in one of its typical dilemmas (to be treated further under Section 8) of intellect and economics has attempted to transform the enemy from the viewpoint of economics into a competitor and from the intellectual point into a debating adversary. In the domain of economics there are no enemies, only competitors, and in a thoroughly moral and ethical world perhaps only debating adversaries. It is irrelevant here whether one rejects, accepts, or perhaps finds it an atavistic remnant of barbaric times that nations continue to group themselves according to friend and enemy, or hopes that the antithesis will one day vanish from the world, or whether it is perhaps sound pedagogic reasoning to imagine that enemies no longer exist at all. The concern here is neither with abstractions nor with normative ideals, but with inherent reality and the real possibility of such a distinction. One may or may not share these hopes and pedagogic ideals. But, rationally speaking, it cannot be denied that nations continue to group themselves according to the friend and enemy antithesis, that the distinction still remains actual today, and that this is an ever present possibility for every people existing in the political sphere.

The enemy is not merely any competitor or just any partner of a conflict in general. He is also not the private adversary whom one hates. An enemy exists only when, at least potentially, one fighting collectivity of people confronts a similar collectivity. The enemy is solely the public enemy, because everything that has a relationship to such a collectivity of men, particularly to a whole nation, becomes public by virtue of such a relationship. The enemy is *hostis,* not *inimicus* in the broader sense; πολέμιος, not ἐχϑρός.[9]

[9] In his *Republic* (Bk. V, Ch. XVI, 470) Plato strongly emphasizes the contrast between the public enemy (πολέμιος) and the private one (ἐχϑρός), but in connection with the other antithesis of war (πόλεμος) and insurrec-

As German and other languages do not distinguish between the private and political enemy, many misconceptions and falsifications are possible. The often quoted "Love your enemies" (Matt. 5:44; Luke 6:27) reads "diligite inimicos vestros," ἀγαπᾶτε τοὺς ἐχϑροὺς ὑμῶν, and not *diligite hostes vestros*. No mention is made of the political enemy. Never in the thousand-year struggle between Christians and Moslems did it occur to a Christian to surrender rather than defend Europe out of love toward the Saracens or Turks. The enemy in the political sense need not be hated personally, and in the private sphere only does it make sense to love one's enemy, i.e., one's adversary. The Bible quotation touches the political antithesis even less than it intends to dissolve, for example, the antithesis of good and evil or beautiful and ugly. It certainly does not mean that one should love and support the enemies of one's own people.

The political is the most intense and extreme antagonism, and every concrete antagonism becomes that much more political the closer it approaches the most extreme point, that of the friend-enemy grouping. In its entirety the state as an organized political entity

---

tion, upheaval, rebellion, civil war (στάσις).* Real war for Plato is a war between Hellenes and Barbarians only (those who are "by nature enemies"), whereas conflicts among Hellenes are for him discords (στάσεις). The thought expressed here is that a people cannot wage war against itself and a civil war is only a self-laceration and it does not signify that perhaps a new state or even a new people is being created. Cited mostly for the *hostis* concept is Pomponius in the *Digest* 50, 16, 118. The most clear-cut definition with additional supporting material is in Forcellini's *Lexicon totius latinitatis* (1965 ed.), II, 684: "A public enemy (*hostis*) is one with whom we are at war publicly. . . . In this respect he differs from a private enemy. He is a person with whom we have private quarrels. They may also be distinguished as follows: a private enemy is a person who hates us, whereas a public enemy is a person who fights against us."

* *Stasis* also means the exact opposite, i.e., peace and order. The dialectic inherent in the term is pointed out by Carl Schmitt in *Politische Theologie II: Die Legende von der Erledigung jeder Politischen Theologie* (Berlin: Duncker & Humblot, 1970), pp. 117–118.

decides for itself the friend-enemy distinction. Furthermore, next to the primary political decisions and under the protection of the decision taken, numerous secondary concepts of the political emanate. As to the equation of politics and state discussed under Section 1, it has the effect, for example, of contrasting a political attitude of a state with party politics so that one can speak of a state's domestic religious, educational, communal, social policy, and so on. Notwithstanding, the state encompasses and relativizes all these antitheses. However an antithesis and antagonism remain here within the state's domain which have relevance for the concept of the political.[10] Finally even more banal forms of politics appear, forms which assume parasite- and caricature-like configurations. What remains here from the original friend-enemy grouping is only some sort of antagonistic moment, which manifests itself in all sorts of tactics and practices, competitions and intrigues; and the most peculiar dealings and manipulations are called politics. But the fact that the substance of the political is contained in the context of a concrete antagonism is still expressed in everyday language, even where the awareness of the extreme case has been entirely lost.

This becomes evident in daily speech and can be exemplified by two obvious phenomena. First, all political concepts, images, and terms have a polemical meaning. They are focused on a specific conflict and are bound to a concrete situation; the result (which manifests itself in war or revolution) is a friend-enemy grouping, and they turn into empty and ghostlike abstractions when this situation disappears. Words such as state, republic,[11] society, class, as well

[10] A social policy existed ever since a politically noteworthy class put forth its social demands; welfare care, which in early times was administered to the poor and distressed, had not been considered a sociopolitical problem and was also not called such. Likewise a church policy existed only where a church constituted a politically significant counterforce.

[11] Machiavelli, for example, calls all nonmonarchical states republics, and his definition is still accepted today. Richard Thoma defines democracy as a nonprivileged state; hence all nondemocracies are classified as privileged states.

as sovereignty, constitutional state, absolutism, dictatorship, economic planning, neutral or total state, and so on, are incomprehensible if one does not know exactly who is to be affected, combated, refuted, or negated by such a term.[12] Above all the polemical character de-

[12] Numerous forms and degrees of intensity of the polemical character are also here possible. But the essentially polemical nature of the politically charged terms and concepts remain nevertheless recognizable. Terminological questions become thereby highly political. A word or expression can simultaneously be reflex, signal, password, and weapon in a hostile confrontation. For example, Karl Renner, a socialist of the Second International, in a very significant scholarly publication, *Die Rechtsinstitute des Privatrechts* (Tübingen: J. C. B. Mohr [Paul Siebeck], 1929), p. 97, calls rent which the tenant pays the landlord "tribute." Most German professors of jurisprudence, judges, and lawyers, would consider such a designation an inadmissible politicalization of civil law relationships and would reject this on the grounds that it would disturb the purely juristic, purely legal, purely scientific discussion. For them the question has been decided in a legal positivist manner, and the therein residing political design of the state is thus recognized. On the other hand, many socialists of the Second International put much value in calling the payments which armed France imposes upon disarmed Germany not "tribute," but "reparations." "Reparation" appears to be more juristic, more legal, more peaceful, less polemical, and more apolitical than "tribute." In scrutinizing this more closely, however, it may be seen that "reparation" is more highly charged and therefore also political because this term is utilized politically to condemn juristically and even morally the vanquished enemy. The imposed payments have the effect of disqualifying and subjugating him not only legally but also morally. The question in Germany today is whether one should say "tribute" or "reparation." This has turned into an internal dispute. In previous centuries a controversy existed between the German kaiser (and king of Hungary) and the Turkish sultan on the question of whether the payments made by the kaiser to the sultan were in the nature of a "pension" or "tribute." The debtor stressed that he did not pay "tribute" but "pension," whereas the creditor considered it to be "tribute." In the relations between Christians and Turks the words were still used in those days more openly and more objectively, and the juristic concepts perhaps had not yet become to the same extent as today political instruments of coercion. Nevertheless, Bodin, who mentions this controversy (*Les Six Livres de la République*, Paris, 1580, p. 784), adds that in most instances "pension"

termines the use of the word political regardless of whether the
adversary is designated as nonpolitical (in the sense of harmless), or
vice versa if one wants to disqualify or denounce him as political in
order to portray oneself as nonpolitical (in the sense of purely scientific, purely moral, purely juristic, purely aesthetic, purely economic,
or on the basis of similar purities) and thereby superior.

Secondly, in usual domestic polemics the word political is
today often used interchangeably with party politics. The inevitable
lack of objectivity in political decisions, which is only the reflex to
suppress the politically inherent friend-enemy antithesis, manifests
itself in the regrettable forms and aspects of the scramble for office
and the politics of patronage. The demand for depoliticalization
which arises in this context means only the rejection of party politics,
etc. The equation politics = party politics is possible whenever
antagonisms among domestic political parties succeed in weakening
the all-embracing political unit, the state. The intensification of
internal antagonisms has the effect of weakening the common
identity vis-à-vis another state. If domestic conflicts among political
parties have become the sole political difference, the most extreme
degree of internal political tension is thereby reached; i.e., the
domestic, not the foreign friend-and-enemy groupings are decisive
for armed conflict. The ever present possibility of conflict must
always be kept in mind. If one wants to speak of politics in the
context of the primacy of internal politics, then this conflict no
longer refers to war between organized nations but to civil war.

For to the enemy concept belongs the ever present possibility
of combat. All peripherals must be left aside from this term, including military details and the development of weapons technology.
War is armed combat between organized political entities; civil war
is armed combat within an organized unit. A self-laceration en-
dangers the survival of the latter. The essence of a weapon is that

is paid not to protect oneself from other enemies, but primarily from the
protector himself and to ransom oneself from an invasion (*pour se racheter
de l'invasion*).

it is a means of physically killing human beings. Just as the term enemy, the word combat, too, is to be understood in its original existential sense. It does not mean competition, nor does it mean pure intellectual controversy nor symbolic wrestlings in which, after all, every human being is somehow always involved, for it is a fact that the entire life of a human being is a struggle and every human being symbolically a combatant. The friend, enemy, and combat concepts receive their real meaning precisely because they refer to the real possibility of physical killing. War follows from enmity. War is the existential negation of the enemy.* It is the most extreme consequence of enmity. It does not have to be common, normal, something ideal, or desirable. But it must nevertheless remain a real possibility for as long as the concept of the enemy remains valid.

It is by no means as though the political signifies nothing but devastating war and every political deed a military action, by no means as though every nation would be uninterruptedly faced with the friend-enemy alternative vis-à-vis every other nation. And, after all, could not the politically reasonable course reside in avoiding war? The definition of the political suggested here neither favors war nor militarism, neither imperialism nor pacifism. Nor is it an attempt to idealize the victorious war or the successful revolution as a "social ideal," since neither war nor revolution is something social or something ideal.[13] The military battle itself is not the

* Schmitt clearly alludes here to the foe concept in politics.

[13] Rudolf Stammler's thesis, which is rooted in neo-Kantian thought, that the "social ideal" is the "community of free willing individuals" is contradicted by Erich Kaufmann in *Das Wesen des Völkerrechts und die clausula rebus sic stantibus* (Tübingen: J. C. B. Mohr [Paul Siebeck], 1911), p. 146, who maintains that "not the community of free willing individuals, but the victorious war is the social ideal: the victorious war as the last means toward that lofty goal" (the participation and self-assertion of the state in world history). This sentence incorporates the typical neo-Kantian liberal notion of "social ideal." But wars, including victorious wars, are something completely incommensurable and incompatible with this conception. This idea is then joined to the notion of the victorious war, which has its habitat in the

"continuation of politics by other means" as the famous term of Clausewitz is generally incorrectly cited.[14] War has its own strategic, tactical, and other rules and points of view, but they all presuppose that the political decision has already been made as to who the enemy is. In war the adversaries most often confront each other openly; normally they are identifiable by a uniform, and the distinction of friend and enemy is therefore no longer a political problem which the fighting soldier has to solve. A British diplomat correctly stated in this context that the politician is better schooled for the battle than the soldier, because the politician fights his whole life whereas the soldier does so in exceptional circumstances only. War is neither the aim nor the purpose nor even the very content of politics. But as an ever present possibility it is the leading presupposition which determines in a characteristic way human action and thinking and thereby creates a specifically political behavior.

The criterion of the friend-and-enemy distinction in no way implies that one particular nation must forever be the friend or enemy of another specific nation or that a state of neutrality is not

Hegelian-Rankian philosophy of history, in which social ideals do not exist. The antithesis which appears at first glance to be striking thus breaks into two disparate parts, and the rhetorical force of a thunderous contrast can neither veil the structural incoherence nor heal the intellectual breach.

[14] Carl von Clausewitz (*Vom Kriege*, 2nd ed. [Berlin: Ferd. Dümmlers Verlagsbuchandlung, 1853], Vol. III, Part III, p. 120) says: "War is nothing but a continuation of political intercourse with a mixture of other means." War is for him a "mere instrument of politics." This cannot be denied, but its meaning for the understanding of the essence of politics is thereby still not exhausted. To be precise, war, for Clausewitz, is not merely one of many instruments, but the *ultima ratio* of the friend-and-enemy grouping. War has its own grammar (i.e., special military-technical laws), but politics remains its brain. It does not have its own logic. This can only be derived from the friend-and-enemy concept, and the sentence on page 121 reveals this core of politics: "If war belongs to politics, it will thereby assume its character. The more grandiose and powerful it becomes, so will also the war, and this may be carried to the point at which war reaches its absolute form. . . ."

possible or could not be politically reasonable. As with every political concept, the neutrality concept too is subject to the ultimate presupposition of a real possibility of a friend-and-enemy grouping. Should only neutrality prevail in the world, then not only war but also neutrality would come to an end. The politics of avoiding war terminates, as does all politics, whenever the possibility of fighting disappears. What always matters is the possibility of the extreme case taking place, the real war, and the decision whether this situation has or has not arrived.

That the extreme case appears to be an exception does not negate its decisive character but confirms it all the more. To the extent that wars today have decreased in number and frequency, they have proportionately increased in ferocity. War is still today the most extreme possibility. One can say that the exceptional case has an especially decisive meaning which exposes the core of the matter. For only in real combat is revealed the most extreme consequence of the political grouping of friend and enemy. From this most extreme possibility human life derives its specifically political tension.

A world in which the possibility of war is utterly eliminated, a completely pacified globe, would be a world without the distinction of friend and enemy and hence a world without politics. It is conceivable that such a world might contain many very interesting antitheses and contrasts, competitions and intrigues of every kind, but there would not be a meaningful antithesis whereby men could be required to sacrifice life, authorized to shed blood, and kill other human beings. For the definition of the political, it is here even irrelevant whether such a world without politics is desirable as an ideal situation. The phenomenon of the political can be understood only in the context of the ever present possibility of the friend-and-enemy grouping, regardless of the aspects which this possibility implies for morality, aesthetics, and economics.

War as the most extreme political means discloses the possibility which underlies every political idea, namely, the distinction of friend and enemy. This makes sense only as long as this distinction in mankind is actually present or at least potentially possible. On the other hand, it would be senseless to wage war for purely religious, purely moral, purely juristic, or purely economic motives. The friend-and-enemy grouping and therefore also war cannot be derived from these specific antitheses of human endeavor. A war need be neither something religious nor something morally good nor something lucrative. War today is in all likelihood none of these. This obvious point is mostly confused by the fact that religious, moral, and other antitheses can intensify to political ones and can bring about the decisive friend-or-enemy constellation. If, in fact, this occurs, then the relevant antithesis is no longer purely religious, moral, or economic, but political. The sole remaining question then is always whether such a friend-and-enemy grouping is really at hand, regardless of which human motives are sufficiently strong to have brought it about.

Nothing can escape this logical conclusion of the political. If pacifist hostility toward war were so strong as to drive pacifists into a war against nonpacifists, in a war against war, that would prove that pacifism truly possesses political energy because it is sufficiently strong to group men according to friend and enemy. If, in fact, the will to abolish war is so strong that it no longer shuns war, then it has become a political motive, i.e., it affirms, even if only as an extreme possibility, war and even the reason for war. Presently this appears to be a peculiar way of justifying wars. The war is then considered to constitute the absolute last war of humanity. Such a war is necessarily unusually intense and inhuman because, by transcending the limits of the political framework, it simultaneously degrades the enemy into moral and other categories and is forced to make of him a monster that must not only be defeated but also utterly destroyed. In other words, he is an enemy who no longer must be compelled to retreat into his borders only.* The feasibility of such war is particularly illustrative of the fact that war as a real

---

* Also here Schmitt clearly alludes to the enemy-foe distinction.

possibility is still present today, and this fact is crucial for the friend-and-enemy antithesis and for the recognition of politics.

4

Every religious, moral, economic, ethical, or other antithesis transforms into a political one if it is sufficiently strong to group human beings effectively according to friend and enemy. The political does not reside in the battle itself, which possesses its own technical, psychological, and military laws, but in the mode of behavior which is determined by this possibility, by clearly evaluating the concrete situation and thereby being able to distinguish correctly the real friend and the real enemy. A religious community which wages wars against members of other religious communities or engages in other wars is already more than a religious community; it is a political entity. It is a political entity when it possesses, even if only negatively, the capacity of promoting that decisive step, when it is in the position of forbidding its members to participate in wars, i.e., of decisively denying the enemy quality of a certain adversary. The same holds true for an association of individuals based on economic interests as, for example, an industrial concern or a labor union. Also a class in the Marxian sense ceases to be something purely economic and becomes a political factor when it reaches this decisive point, for example, when Marxists approach the class struggle seriously and treat the class adversary as a real enemy and fights him either in the form of a war of state against state or in a civil war within a state. The real battle is then of necessity no longer fought according to economic laws but has—next to the fighting methods in the narrowest technical sense—its political necessities and orientations, coalitions and compromises, and so on. Should the proletariat succeed in seizing political power within a state, a proletarian state will thus have been created. This state is by no means less of a political power than a national state, a theocratic, mercantile, or soldier state, a civil service state, or some other type of political entity. Were it possible to group all mankind in the proletarian and bourgeois antithesis, as friend and enemy in proletarian and capitalist states, and if, in the process, all other friend-and-enemy groupings were to disappear, the total reality of the political would then be revealed, insofar as concepts, which at first glance had appeared to be purely economic, turn into political ones. If the political power of a class or of some other group within a state is sufficiently strong to hinder the waging of wars against other states but incapable of assuming or lacking the will to assume the state's power and thereby decide on the friend-and-enemy distinction and, if necessary, make war, then the political entity is destroyed.

The political can derive its energy from the most varied human endeavors, from the religious, economic, moral, and other antitheses. It does not describe its own substance, but only the intensity of an association or dissociation of human beings whose motives can be religious, national (in the ethnic or cultural sense), economic, or of another kind and can effect at different times different coalitions and separations. The real friend-enemy grouping is existentially so strong and decisive that the nonpolitical antithesis, at precisely the moment at which it becomes political, pushes aside and subordinates its hitherto purely religious, purely economic, purely cultural criteria and motives to the conditions and conclusions of the political situation at hand. In any event, that grouping is always political which orients itself toward this most extreme possibility. This grouping is therefore always the decisive human grouping, the political entity. If such an entity exists at all, it is always the decisive entity, and it is sovereign in the sense that the decision about the critical situation, even if it is the exception, must always necessarily reside there.

A valid meaning is here attached to the word sovereignty, just as to the term entity. Both do not at all imply that a political entity must necessarily determine every aspect of a person's life or that a centralized system should destroy every other organization or corporation.* It may be that economic considerations can be stronger than anything desired by a government which is ostensibly indifferent toward economics. Likewise, religious convictions can easily determine the politics of an allegedly neutral state. What always matters is only the possibility of conflict. If, in fact, the economic, cultural, or religious counterforces are so strong that they are in a position to decide upon the extreme possibility from their viewpoint, then these forces have in actuality become the new substance of the political entity. It would be an indication that these counterforces had not reached the decisive point in the political if they turned out to be not sufficiently powerful to prevent a war contrary to their interests or principles. Should the counterforces be strong enough to hinder a war desired by the state that was contrary to their interests or principles but not sufficiently capable themselves of deciding about war, then a unified political entity would no longer exist. However one may look at it, in the orientation toward the possible extreme case of an actual battle against a real enemy, the political entity is essential, and it is the decisive entity for the friend-or-enemy grouping; and in this (and not in any kind of absolutist sense), it is sovereign. Otherwise the political entity is nonexistent.

When the political significance of domestic economic associations had been recognized, in particular the growth of labor unions, the laws of the state appeared quite powerless against their economic weapon, the strike. Consequently, some have somewhat hastily proclaimed the death and the end of the state. As far as I can tell this emerged as a doctrine of the French syndicalists after 1906 and 1907.[15] Duguit is in this context the best known political theorist.

* Schmitt has consistently maintained this idea and thus has never entertained the thought of a totalitarian state. See Schwab, *The Challenge*, pp. 146–148.

[15] "This enormous thing . . . the death of this fantastic, prodigious being which held such a colossal place in history: the state is dead." E. Berth, whose ideas stem from Georges Sorel, in *Le Mouvement socialiste*, October 1907, p. 314. Léon Duguit cites this in his lectures *Le Droit social, le droit*

Ever since 1901 he has tried to refute the conception of sovereignty and the conception of the personality of the state with some accurate arguments against an uncritical metaphysics of the state and personifications of the state, which are, after all, only remnants from the world of princely absolutism but in essence miss the actual political meaning of the concept of sovereignty. Similarly, this also holds true for G. D. H. Cole's and Harold Laski's so-called theory of pluralism, which appeared somewhat later in the Anglo-Saxon world.[16] Their pluralism * consists in denying the sovereignty of the

individuel et la transformation de l'État, 1st ed. (Paris: Felix Alcan, 1908). He considered it sufficient to say that the sovereign state conceived as a person is dead or at the point of dying (p. 150: "L'État personnel et souverain . . . est mort ou sur le point de mourir"). Such sentences are not found in Duguit's *L'État* (Paris: Thorin et Fils, 1901), although the critique of the sovereignty concept is already the same. Interesting additional examples of this syndicalist diagnosis of the contemporary state appear in A. Esmein's *Éléments de droit constitutionnel* (7th ed., ed. H. Nézard [Paris: Sirey, 1921], I, 55 ff.), and above all in the particularly interesting book by Maxime Leroy, *Les Transformations de la puissance publique* (Paris: V. Giard & Brière, 1907). With respect to its diagnosis of the state, the syndicalist doctrine is also to be distinguished from the Marxist construction. For the Marxists the state is not dead or at the point of dying. The state is rather a means for bringing about classes and necessary to make the classless and then the stateless society. But in the meantime this state is still real, and precisely with the aid of Marxist doctrine it has received new energies and new life in the Soviet Union.

[16] A survey and plausible assemblage of Cole's theses (formulated by him) is reprinted in the *Proceedings of the Aristotelian Society,* XVI (1916), 310–325. The central thesis here is also that states are equal to other kinds of human associations. The following works by Laski are mentioned: *Studies in the Problem of Sovereignty* (1917), *Authority in the Modern State* (1919), *Foundations of Sovereignty* (1921), *A Grammar of Politics* (1925), "Das Recht und der Staat," *Zeitschrift für öffentliches Recht,* X (1931), 1–27; also, Kung Chuan Hsiao, *Political Pluralism* (London: K. Paul, Trench,

* As far as the translator can gather, the Anglo-Saxon theory of pluralism was unknown in Germany until Schmitt called attention to it.

political entity by stressing time and again that the individual lives in numerous different social entities and associations. He is a member of a religious institution, nation, labor union, family, sports club, and many other associations. These control him in differing degrees from case to case, and impose on him a cluster of obligations in such a way that no one of these associations can be said to be decisive and sovereign. On the contrary, each one in a different field may prove to be the strongest, and then the conflict of loyalties can only be resolved from case to case. It is conceivable, for example, that a labor union should decide to order its members no longer to attend church, but in spite of it they continue to do so, and that simultaneously a demand by the church that members leave the labor union remains likewise unheeded.

Particularly striking in this example is the co-ordination of religious associations and labor unions, which could result in an alliance because of their common antipathy toward the state. This is typical of the pluralism which appears in the Anglo-Saxon countries. Its main theoretical point of departure was, next to Gierke's association theory, J. Neville Figgis' book on churches in the modern state.[17] The historical context to which Laski always returns and

---

Trubner & Co., Ltd., 1927). For a critique of this pluralism see W. Y. Elliott, "The Pragmatic Politics of Mr. H. J. Laski," *The American Political Science Review*, XVIII (1924), 251–275; *The Pragmatic Revolt in Politics* (New York: The Macmillan Co., 1928), and Carl Schmitt, "Staatsethik und pluralistischer Staat," *Kant-Studien*, XXXV (1930), 28–42. On the pluralist splintering of the contemporary German state and the development of parliament into a showcase of a pluralist system see Carl Schmitt, *Der Hüter der Verfassung* (Tübingen: J. C. B. Mohr [Paul Siebeck], 1931; Berlin; Duncker & Humblot, 1969), pp. 73 ff.

[17] Figgis, *Churches in the Modern State* (London: Longmans, Green and Co., 1913) noted on p. 249 that Maitland, whose legal historical researches likewise influenced the pluralists, considered Gierke's *Das deutsche Genossenschaftsrecht* "to be the greatest book he had ever read" and remarked that the medieval controversy between church and empire, i.e., between pope and emperor, or more precisely between the spiritual order and the temporal ones, was not a controversy of two societies but a civil war within the same

which obviously made a great impression on him is the simultane-
ous and equally unsuccessful attacks of Bismarck against the Catholic Church and the socialists. In the *Kulturkampf* against the
Roman Church it was seen that even a state of the unimpaired
strength of Bismarck's Reich was not absolutely sovereign and
powerful. This state was equally unsuccessful in its battle against
the socialist working class. Would this state have been sufficiently
strong in the economic domain to remove from the labor unions
their power to strike?

This critique is largely justified. The juridic formulas of the
omnipotence of the state are, in fact, only superficial secularizations
of theological formulas of the omnipotence of God.* Also, the nineteenth-century German doctrine of the personality of the state is

social entity. But today two societies, *duo populi,* face one another. This in
my opinion is correct. In the period prior to the schism the relation of pope
and emperor could still be understood according to the formula that the pope
possessed the *auctoritas* and the emperor the *potestas.* Accordingly a division
existed within the same entity, and Catholic doctrine since the twelfth century has maintained that church and state are two *societates,* and indeed both
are *societates perfectae* (each one sovereign and autarchic in its own domain).
Naturally on the side of the Church the Catholics recognized their church
only as *societas perfecta,* whereas on the side of the state today a plurality
of *societates perfectae* appear, whose perfection, considering the great number, becomes very problematical. An extraordinarily clear summary of Catholic doctrine is contained in Paul Simon's "Staat und Kirche," *Deutsches
Volkstum* (August 1931), pp. 576–596. The co-ordination of churches and
labor unions which is typical of the Anglo-Saxon pluralist notion is naturally
unthinkable in Catholic theory, and it is just as inconceivable for the Catholic
Church to permit itself to be treated on an equal level with an international
labor union. In reality the Church serves Laski, as Elliott aptly remarked,
only as a "stalking horse" for the labor unions. A clear and fundamental
debate on the two theories and their mutual relations is unfortunately missing
so far on the side of the Catholics as well as on the part of the pluralists.

    * As early as 1922 Schmitt asserted that "all significant concepts of
the theory of the modern state are secularized theological concepts." *Politische
Theologie: Vier Kapitel zur Lehre von der Souveränität* (Munich: Duncker &
Humblot, 1922, 1934), p. 49.

important here because it was in part a polemical antithesis to the personality of the absolute prince, and in part to a state considered as a higher third (vis-à-vis all other social groups) with the aim of evading the dilemma of monarchical or popular sovereignty. But the question remains unanswered: which social entity (if I am permitted to use here the imprecise liberal concept of "social") decides the extreme case and determines the decisive friend-and-enemy grouping? Neither a church nor a labor union nor an alliance of both could have forbidden or prevented a war which the German Reich might have wanted to wage under Bismarck. He could not declare war against the pope, but only because the pope no longer possessed the *jus belli;* and also the socialist labor unions did not want to appear in the role of a *partie belligérante.* In any event, no organized opposition then imaginable could have possibly deprived the German government of making the relevant decision in the extreme case; such an opposition would have risked being treated as an enemy and would thus have been affected by all the consequences of this concept. Furthermore, neither the Church nor a labor union was prepared to engage in a civil war.[18] These considerations are sufficient to establish a reasonable concept of sovereignty and entity. The political entity is by its very nature the decisive entity, regardless of the sources from which it derives its

[18] Because Laski also refers to the controversy of the English Catholics with Gladstone, the following sentences are cited here from Cardinal John Henry Newman's letter to the Duke of Norfolk [regarding Gladstone's *The Vatican Decrees in Their Bearing on Civil Allegiance* (1874)]: "Suppose England were to send her Ironclads to support Italy against the Pope and his allies, English Catholics would be very indignant, they would take part with the Pope before the war began, they would use all constitutional means to hinder it; but who believes that, when they were once in the war, their action would be anything else than prayers and exertions for a termination of it? What reason is there for saying that they would commit themselves to any step of a treasonable nature . . . ?" *A Letter Addressed to His Grace the Duke of Norfolk* (New York: The Catholic Publication Society, 1875), p. 64.

last psychic motives. It exists or does not exist. If it exists, it is the supreme, that is, in the decisive case, the authoritative entity.

That the state is an entity and in fact the decisive entity rests upon its political character. A pluralist theory is either the theory of state which arrives at the unity of state by a federalism of social associations or a theory of the dissolution or rebuttal of the state. If, in fact, it challenges the entity and places the political association on an equal level with the others, for example, religious or economic associations, it must, above all, answer the question as to the specific content of the political. Although in his numerous books Laski speaks of state, politics, sovereignty, and government, one does not find in these a specific definition of the political. The state simply transforms itself into an association which competes with other associations; it becomes a society among some other societies which exist within or outside the state. That is the pluralism of this theory of state. Its entire ingenuity is directed against earlier exaggerations of the state, against its majesty and its personality, against its claim to possess the monopoly of the highest unity, while it remains unclear what, according to this pluralist theory of state, the political entity should be. At times it appears in its old liberal form, as a mere servant of the essentially economically determined society, at times pluralistically as a distinct type of society, that is, as one association among other associations, at times as the product of a federalism of social associations or an umbrella association of a conglomeration of associations. Above all, it has to be explained why human beings should have to form a governmental association in addition to the religious, cultural, economic, and other associations, and what would be its specific political meaning. No clear chain of thought is discernible here. What appears finally is an all-embracing, monistically global, and by no means pluralist concept, namely Cole's "society" and Laski's "humanity."

The pluralist theory of state is in itself pluralistic, that is, it has no center but draws its thoughts from rather different intellectual circles (religion, economics, liberalism, socialism, etc.). It ignores the central concept of every theory of state, the political, and does not even mention the possibility that the pluralism of associations could lead to a federally constructed political entity. It totally revolves in a liberal individualism. The result is nothing else than a revocable service for individuals and their free associations. One association is played off against another and all questions and conflicts are decided by individuals. In reality there exists no political society or association but only one political entity—one political community. The ever present possibility of a friend-and-enemy grouping suffices to forge a decisive entity which transcends the mere societal-associational groupings. The political entity is something specifically different, and vis-à-vis other associations, something decisive.[19] Were this entity to disappear, even if only potentially, then the political itself would disappear. Only as long as the essence of the political is not comprehended or not taken into consideration is it possible to place a political association pluralistically on the same level with religious, cultural, economic, or other associations and permit it to compete with these. As we shall attempt to show below (Section 6), the concept of the political yields pluralistic consequences, but not in the sense that, within one and the same political entity, instead of the decisive friend-and-enemy grouping, a pluralism could take its place without destroying the entity and the political itself.

5

To the state as an essentially political entity belongs the *jus belli*, i.e., the real possibility of deciding in a concrete situation upon the enemy and the ability to fight him with the power emanating from the entity. As long as a politically united people is prepared

[19] "We can say that on the day of mobilization the hitherto existing society was transformed into a community." E. Lederer, "Zur Soziologie des Weltkriegs," *Archiv für Sozialwissenschaft und Sozialpolitik,* 39 (1915), p. 349.

to fight for its existence, independence, and freedom on the basis
of a decision emanating from the political entity, this specifically
political question has primacy over the technical means by which
the battle will be waged, the nature of the army's organization, and
what the prospects are for winning the war. The development of
military techniques appears to move in a direction which will
perhaps permit only a few states to survive, i.e., those whose industrial potential would allow them to wage a promising war. Should
smaller and weaker states be unable to maintain their independence
by virtue of an appropriate alliance, they may then be forced, voluntarily or by necessity, to abdicate the *jus belli*. This development
would still not prove that war, state, and politics will altogether
cease. The numerous changes and revolutions in human history
and development have produced new forms and dimensions of
political groupings. Previously existing political structures were destroyed, new kinds of foreign and civil wars arose, and the number
of organized political entities soon increased or diminished.

The state as the decisive political entity possesses an enormous
power: the possibility of waging war and thereby publicly disposing
of the lives of men. The *jus belli* contains such a disposition. It
implies a double possibility: the right to demand from its own
members the readiness to die and unhesitatingly to kill enemies.
The endeavor of a normal state consists above all in assuring total
peace within the state and its territory. To create tranquility, security, and order and thereby establish the normal situation is the
prerequisite for legal norms to be valid. Every norm presupposes a
normal situation, and no norm can be valid in an entirely abnormal
situation.

As long as the state is a political entity this requirement for
internal peace compels it in critical situations to decide also upon
the domestic enemy. Every state provides, therefore, some kind of
formula for the declaration of an internal enemy. The πολέμιος
declaration in the public law of the Greek republics and the *hostis*

declaration in Roman public law are but two examples. Whether the form is sharper or milder, explicit or implicit, whether ostracism, expulsion, proscription, or outlawry are provided for in special laws or in explicit or general descriptions, the aim is always the same, namely to declare an enemy. That, depending on the attitude of those who had been declared enemies of state, is possibly the sign of civil war, i.e., the dissolution of the state as an organized political entity, internally peaceful, territorially enclosed, and impenetrable to aliens. The civil war then decides the further fate of this entity. More so than for other states, this is particularly valid for a constitutional state, despite all the constitutional ties to which the state is bound. In a constitutional state, as Lorenz von Stein says, the constitution is "the expression of the societal order, the existence of society itself. As soon as it is attacked the battle must then be waged outside the constitution and the law, hence decided by the power of weapons." *

The authority to decide, in the form of a verdict on life and death, the *jus vitae ac necis,* can also belong to another nonpolitical order within the political entity, for instance, to the family or to the head of the household, but not the right of a *hostis* declaration as long as the political entity is an actuality and possesses the *jus belli.* If a political entity exists at all, the right of vendettas between families or kinsfolk would have to be suspended at least temporarily during a war. A human group which renounces these consequences of a political entity ceases to be a political group, because it thereby renounces the possibility of deciding whom it considers to be the enemy and how he should be treated. By virtue of this power over the physical life of men, the political community transcends all other associations or societies. Within the community, however, subordinate groupings of a secondary political nature could exist with

* Omitted here is a long note by Schmitt on examples of enemy declaration. The Lorenz von Stein citation is from his *Geschichte der sozialen Bewegung in Frankreich,* I, *Der Begriff der Gesellschaft,* ed. G. Salomon (Munich: Drei Masken Verlag, 1921), p. 494.

their own or transferred rights, even with a limited *jus vitae ac necis* over members of smaller groups.

A religious community, a church, can exhort a member to die for his belief and become a martyr, but only for the salvation of his own soul, not for the religious community in its quality as an earthly power; otherwise it assumes a political dimension. Its holy wars and crusades are actions which presuppose an enemy decision, just as do other wars. Under no circumstances can anyone demand that any member of an economically determined society, whose order in the economic domain is based upon rational procedures, sacrifice his life in the interest of rational operations. To justify such a demand on the basis of economic expediency would contradict the individualistic principles of a liberal economic order and could never be justified by the norms or ideals of an economy autonomously conceived. The individual may voluntarily die for whatever reason he may wish. That is, like everything in an essentially individualist liberal society, a thoroughly private matter—decided upon freely.

The economically functioning society possesses sufficient means to neutralize nonviolently, in a "peaceful" fashion, those economic competitors who are inferior, unsuccessful or mere "perturbers." Concretely speaking, this implies that this competitor will be left to starve if he does not voluntarily accommodate himself. A purely cultural or civilized system of society will not lack social indications to rid itself of unwanted perturbations or unwanted additions. But no program, no ideal, no norm, no expediency confers a right to dispose of the physical life of other human beings. To demand seriously of human beings that they kill others and be prepared to die themselves so that trade and industry may flourish for the survivors or that the purchasing power of grandchildren may grow is sinister and crazy. It is a manifest fraud to condemn war as homicide and then demand of men that they wage war, kill and be killed, so that there will never again be war. War, the readiness of combatants to die, the physical killing of human beings who belong on the side of the enemy—all this has no normative meaning, but an existential meaning only, particularly in a real combat situation with a real enemy. There exists no rational purpose, no norm no matter how true, no program no matter how exemplary, no social ideal no matter how beautiful, no legitimacy nor legality which could justify men in killing each other for this reason. If such physical destruction of human life is not motivated by an existential threat to one's own way of life, then it cannot be justified. Just as little can war be justified by ethical and juristic norms. If there really are enemies in the existential sense as meant here, then it is justified, but only politically, to repel and fight them physically.

That justice does not belong to the concept of war has been generally recognized since Grotius.[20] The notions which postulate a just war usually serve a political purpose. To demand of a politically united people that it wage war for a just cause only is either something self-evident, if it means that war can be risked only against a real enemy, or it is a hidden political aspiration of some other party to wrest from the state its *jus belli* and to find norms of justice whose content and application in the concrete case is not decided upon by the state but by another party, and thereby it determines who the enemy is. For as long as a people exists in the political sphere, this people must, even if only in the most extreme case—and whether this point has been reached has to be decided by it—determine by itself the distinction of friend and enemy. Therein resides the essence of its political existence. When it no longer possesses the capacity or the will to make this distinction, it ceases to exist politically. If it permits this decision to be made by another, then it is no longer a politically free people and is absorbed into another political system. The justification of war does not reside in its being fought for ideals or norms of justice, but in its being fought against a real enemy. All

[20] *De jure belli ac pacis,* Vol. I, Bk. I, Ch. I, #2: "Justice is not included in the definition [i.e., of war]." In the scholasticism of the Middle Ages war against heretics was considered just—a *bellum justum* (accordingly as war, not as execution, peaceful measure or sanction).

confusions of this category of friend and enemy can be explained as results of blendings of some sort of abstractions or norms.

A people which exists in the sphere of the political cannot in case of need renounce the right to determine by itself the friend-and-enemy distinction. It can solemnly declare that it condemns war as a means of solving international disputes and can renounce it as a means of national policy, as was done in the so-called Kellogg Pact of 1928.[21] In so doing it has neither repudiated war as an instrument of international politics (and a war as an instrument of international politics can be worse than a war as an instrument of a national policy only) nor condemned nor outlawed war altogether. Such a declaration is subject, first of all, to specific reservations which are explicitly or implicitly self-understood as, for example, the reservation regarding the autonomous existence of the state and its self-defense, the reservation regarding existing treaties, the right of a continuing free and independent existence, and so on. Second, these reservations are, according to their logical structure, no mere

21. . . . The Kellogg Pact * text of August 27, 1928, contains most important reservations—England's national honor, self-defense, the League Covenant and Locarno, welfare and territorial integrity of territories such as Egypt, Palestine, and so forth; for France: self-defense, League Covenant, Locarno and neutrality treaties, above all the observance of the Kellogg Pact; for Poland: self-defense, observance of the Kellogg Pact, the League Covenant. . . . The general juristic problem of reservations has so far received no systematic treatment, not even there where explicit treatments mention the sanctity of treaties and the sentence *pacta sunt servanda*. To fill this gap a noteworthy beginning is to be found in Carl Bilfinger, "Betrachtungen über politisches Recht," *Zeitschrift für ausländisches öffentliches Recht und Völkerrecht*, I (1929), 57–76. With respect to the general problem of a pacified humanity, see Section 6 below. On the fact that the Kellogg Pact does not outlaw war, but sanctions it, see E. M. Borchard, "The Kellogg Treaties Sanction War," *ibid.*, pp. 126–131, and Arthur Wegner, *Einführung in die Rechtswissenschaft* (Berlin: Walter de Gruyter, 1931), pp. 109–111.

* On the Kellogg Pact see also Carl Schmitt, *Der Nomos der Erde im Völkerrecht des Jus Publicum Europaeum* (Köln: Greven Verlag, 1950; Berlin: Duncker & Humblot, 1974), pp. 255, 272.

exceptions to the norm, but altogether give the norm its concrete content. They are not peripheral but essential exceptions; they give the treaty its real content in dubious cases. Third, as long as a sovereign state exists, this state decides for itself, by virtue of its independence, whether or not such a reservation (self-defense, enemy aggression, violation of existing treaties including the Kellogg Pact, and so on) is or is not given in the concrete case. Fourth, war cannot altogether be outlawed, but only specific individuals, peoples, states, classes, religions, etc., which, by being outlawed, are declared to be the enemy. The solemn declaration of outlawing war does not abolish the friend-enemy distinction, but, on the contrary, opens new possibilities by giving an international *hostis* declaration new content and new vigor.

Were this distinction to vanish then political life would vanish altogether. A people which exists in the political sphere cannot, despite entreating declarations to the contrary, escape from making this fateful distinction. If a part of the population declares that it no longer recognizes enemies, then, depending on the circumstance, it joins their side and aids them. Such a declaration does not abolish the reality of the friend-and-enemy distinction. Quite another question concerns citizens of a state who declare that they personally have no enemies. A private person has no political enemies. Such a declaration can at most say that he would like to place himself outside the political community to which he belongs and continue to live as a private individual only.[22] Furthermore, it would be a mistake to believe that a nation could eliminate the distinction of friend and enemy by declaring its friendship for the entire world

[22] In this case it is a matter for the political community somehow to regulate this kind of nonpublic, politically disinterested existence (by privileges for aliens, internment, exterritoriality, permits of residence and concessions, laws for metics, or in some other way). On aspiring to a life without political risks (definition of the bourgeois) see Hegel's assertion below, Section 7.

or by voluntarily disarming itself. The world will not thereby become depoliticalized, and it will not be transplanted into a condition of pure morality, pure justice, or pure economics. If a people is afraid of the trials and risks implied by existing in the sphere of politics, then another people will appear which will assume these trials by protecting it against foreign enemies and thereby taking over political rule. The protector then decides who the enemy is by virtue of the eternal relation of protection and obedience.

[Schmitt's Note]

On this principle rests the feudal order and the relation of lord and vassal, leader and led, patron and clients. This relation is clearly and explicitly seen here. No form of order, no reasonable legitimacy or legality can exist without protection and obedience. The *protego ergo obligo* is the *cogito ergo sum* of the state. A political theory which does not systematically become aware of this sentence remains an inadequate fragment. Hobbes designated this (at the end of his English edition of 1651, p. 396) as the true purpose of his *Leviathan,* to instill in man once again "the mutual relation between Protection and Obedience"; human nature as well as divine right demands its inviolable observation.

Hobbes himself had experienced this truth in the terrible times of civil war, because then all legitimate and normative illusions with which men like to deceive themselves regarding political realities in periods of untroubled security vanish. If within the state there are organized parties capable of according their members more protection than the state, then the latter becomes at best an annex of such parties, and the individual citizen knows whom he has to obey. As has been shown (under Section 4 above), a pluralistic theory of state can justify this. The fundamental correctness of the protection-obedience axiom comes to the fore even more clearly in foreign policy and interstate relations: the simplest expression of this axiom is found in the protectorate under international law, the federal state, the confederation of states dominated by one of them, and the various kinds of treaties offering protection and guarantees.

———————————— • ————————————

It would be ludicrous to believe that a defenseless people has nothing but friends, and it would be a deranged calculation to suppose that the enemy could perhaps be touched by the absence of a resistance. No one thinks it possible that the world could, for example, be transformed into a condition of pure morality by the renunciation of every aesthetic or economic productivity. Even less can a people hope to bring about a purely moral or purely economic condition of humanity by evading every political decision. If a people no longer possesses the energy or the will to maintain itself in the sphere of politics, the latter will not thereby vanish from the world. Only a weak people will disappear.

6

The political entity presupposes the real existence of an enemy and therefore coexistence with another political entity. As long as a state exists, there will thus always be in the world more than just one state. A world state which embraces the entire globe and all of humanity cannot exist. The political world is a pluriverse, not a universe. In this sense every theory of state is pluralistic, even though in a different way from the domestic theory of pluralism discussed in Section 4. The political entity cannot by its very nature be universal in the sense of embracing all of humanity and the entire world. If the different states, religions, classes, and other human groupings on earth should be so unified that a conflict among them is impossible and even inconceivable and if civil war should forever be foreclosed in a realm which embraces the globe, then the distinction of friend and enemy would also cease. What remains is neither politics nor state, but culture, civilization, economics, morality, law, art, entertainment, etc. If and when this condition will appear, I do not know. At the moment, this is not the case. And it is self-deluding to believe that the termination of a modern war would lead to world peace—thus setting forth the idyllic goal of complete and final depoliticalization—simply because a war between the great powers today may easily turn into a world war.

Humanity as such cannot wage war because it has no enemy, at least not on this planet. The concept of humanity excludes the concept of the enemy, because the enemy does not cease to be a human being—and hence there is no specific differentiation in that concept. That wars are waged in the name of humanity is not a contradiction of this simple truth; quite the contrary, it has an especially intensive political meaning. When a state fights its political enemy in the name of humanity, it is not a war for the sake of humanity, but a war wherein a particular state seeks to usurp a universal concept against its military opponent. At the expense of its opponent, it tries to identify itself with humanity in the same way as one can misuse peace, justice, progress, and civilization in order to claim these as one's own and to deny the same to the enemy.

The concept of humanity is an especially useful ideological instrument of imperialist expansion, and in its ethical-humanitarian form it is a specific vehicle of economic imperialism. Here one is reminded of a somewhat modified expression of Proudhon's: whoever invokes humanity wants to cheat. To confiscate the word humanity, to invoke and monopolize such a term probably has certain incalculable effects, such as denying the enemy the quality of being human and declaring him to be an outlaw of humanity; and a war can thereby be driven to the most extreme inhumanity.[23]

[23] On outlawing war, see above, Section 5. Pufendorf (*De jure naturae et gentium*, VIII, 6, #5) quotes approvingly Bacon's comment that specific peoples are "proscribed by nature itself," e.g., the Indians, because they eat human flesh. And in fact the Indians of North America were then exterminated. As civilization progresses and morality rises, even less harmless things

But besides this highly political utilization of the nonpolitical term humanity, there are no wars of humanity as such. Humanity is not a political concept, and no political entity or society and no status corresponds to it. The eighteenth-century humanitarian concept of humanity was a polemical denial of the then existing aristocratic-feudal system and the privileges accompanying it. Humanity according to natural law and liberal-individualistic doctrines is a universal, i.e., all-embracing, social ideal, a system of relations between individuals. This materializes only when the real possibility of war is precluded and every friend and enemy grouping becomes impossible. In this universal society there would no longer be nations in the form of political entities, no class struggles, and no enemy groupings.

The League of Nations idea was clear and precise as long as such a body could be construed as a polemical antithesis of a league of monarchs. It was in this context that the German word *Völkerbund* originated in the eighteenth century. But this polemical meaning disappeared with the political significance of monarchy. A *Völkerbund* could moreover serve as an ideological instrument of the imperialism of a state or a coalition of states against other states. This would then confirm all that has been said previously concerning the political use of the term humanity. For many people the ideal of a global organization means nothing else than the utopian idea of total depoliticalization. Demands are therefore made, almost always indiscriminately, that all states on earth become members as soon as possible and that it be universal. Universality at any price would necessarily have to mean total depoliticalization and with it, particularly, the nonexistence of states.

As a result of the 1919 Paris peace treaties an incongruous organization came into existence—the Geneva establishment, which is called in German *Völkerbund* (in French, *Société des Nations,*

---

than devouring human flesh could perhaps qualify as deserving to be outlawed in such a manner. Maybe one day it will be enough if a people were unable to pay its debts.

and English, the League of Nations) but should properly be called a society of nations. This body is an organization which presupposes the existence of states, regulates some of their mutual relations, and even guarantees their political existence. It is neither universal nor even an international organization. If the German word for international is used correctly and honestly it must be distinguished from interstate and applied instead to international movements which transcend the borders of states and ignore the territorial integrity, impenetrability, and impermeability of existing states as, for example, the Third International. Immediately exposed here are the elementary antitheses of international and interstate, of a depoliticalized universal society and interstate guarantees of the *status quo* of existing frontiers. It is hard to comprehend how a scholarly treatment of the League of Nations could skirt this and even lend support to this confusion. The Geneva League of Nations does not eliminate the possibility of wars, just as it does not abolish states. It introduces new possibilities for wars, permits wars to take place, sanctions coalition wars, and by legitimizing and sanctioning certain wars it sweeps away many obstacles to war. As it has existed so far, it is under specific circumstances a very useful meeting place, a system of diplomatic conferences which meet under the name of the League of Nations Council and the Assembly of the League of Nations. These bodies are linked to a technical bureau, that of the Secretariat. As I have already shown elsewhere,[24] this establishment is not a league, but possibly an alliance. The genuine concept of humanity is expressed in it only insofar as its actual activities reside in the humanitarian and not in the political field, and only as an interstate administrative community does it at least have a tendency toward a meaningful universality. But in view of the League's true constitution and because this so-called League still enables wars to be fought, even this tendency is an ideal postulate only. A league of nations which is not universal can only be polit-

[24] *Die Kernfrage des Völkerbundes* (Berlin: Ferd. Dümmler, 1926).

ically significant when it represents a potential or actual alliance, i.e., a coalition. The *jus belli* would not thereby be abolished but, more or less, totally or partially, transferred to the alliance. A league of nations as a concrete existing universal human organization would, on the contrary, have to accomplish the difficult task of, first, effectively taking away the *jus belli* from all the still existing human groupings, and, second, simultaneously not assuming the *jus belli* itself. Otherwise, universality, humanity, depoliticalized society—in short, all essential characteristics—would again be eliminated.

Were a world state to embrace the entire globe and humanity, then it would be no political entity and could only be loosely called a state. If, in fact, all humanity and the entire world were to become a unified entity based exclusively on economics and on technically regulating traffic, then it still would not be more of a social entity than a social entity of tenants in a tenement house, customers purchasing gas from the same utility company, or passengers traveling on the same bus. An interest group concerned exclusively with economics or traffic cannot become more than that, in the absence of an adversary. Should that interest group also want to become cultural, ideological, or otherwise more ambitious, and yet remain strictly nonpolitical, then it would be a neutral consumer or producer co-operative moving between the poles of ethics and economics. It would know neither state nor kingdom nor empire, neither republic nor monarchy, neither aristocracy nor democracy, neither protection nor obedience, and would altogether lose its political character.

The acute question to pose is upon whom will fall the frightening power implied in a world-embracing economic and technical organization. This question can by no means be dismissed in the belief that everything would then function automatically, that things would administer themselves, and that a government by people over people would be superfluous because human beings would then be absolutely free. For what would they be free? This can be answered by optimistic or pessimistic conjectures, all of which finally lead to an anthropological profession of faith.

7

One could test all theories of state and political ideas according to their anthropology and thereby classify these as to whether they consciously or unconsciously presuppose man to be by nature evil or by nature good. The distinction is to be taken here in a rather summary fashion and not in any specifically moral or ethical sense. The problematic or unproblematic conception of man is decisive for the presupposition of every further political consideration, the answer to the question whether man is a dangerous being or not, a risky or a harmless creature.

[Schmitt's Note]

The numerous modifications and variations of this anthropological distinction of good and evil are not reviewed here in detail. Evil may appear as corruption, weakness, cowardice, stupidity, or also as brutality, sensuality, vitality, irrationality, and so on. Goodness may appear in corresponding variations as reasonableness, perfectibility, the capacity of being manipulated, of being taught, peaceful, and so forth. Striking in this context is the political significance of animal fables. Almost all can be applied to a real political situation: the problem of aggression in the fable of the wolf and the lamb; the question of guilt for the plague in La Fontaine's fable, a guilt which of course falls upon the donkey; justice between states in the fables of animal assemblies; disarmament in Churchill's election speech of October 1928, which depicts how every animal believes that its teeth, claws, horns are only instruments for maintaining peace; the large fish which devour the small ones, etc. This curious analogy can be explained by the direct connection of political anthropology with what the political philosophers of the seventeenth century (Hobbes, Spinoza, Pufendorf) called the state of nature. In it, states exist among themselves in a condition of continual danger, and their acting subjects are evil for precisely the same reasons as animals who are stirred by their drives (hunger, greediness, fear, jealousy). It is unnecessary to differ with Wilhelm Dilthey: "Man according to Machiavelli is not by nature evil. Some places seem to indicate this. . . . But what Machiavelli wants to express everywhere is that man, if not checked, has an irresistible inclination to slide from passion to evil: animality, drives, passions are the kernels of human nature—above all love and fear. Machiavelli is inexhaustible in his psychological observations of the play of passions. . . . From this principal feature of human nature he derives the fundamental law of all political life." [25] In the chapter "Der Machtmensch" in *Lebensformen* [26] Eduard Spranger says: "For the politician the science of man is naturally of prime interest." It appears to me, however, that Spranger takes too technical a view of this interest, as interest in the tactical manipulation of instinctive drives. In the further elaboration of this chapter, which is crammed full of ideas and observations, there can be recognized time and again the specifically political phenomena and the entire existentiality of the political. For example, the sentence "the dignity of power appears to grow with its sphere of influence" relates to a phenomenon which is rooted in the sphere of the political and can therefore be understood only politically. It is, to be sure, applicable to the following thesis: the weight of the political is determined by the intensity of alignments according to which the decisive associations and dissociations adjust themselves. Also Hegel's proposition concerning the dialectical change of quantity into quality is comprehensible in the context of political thought only (see the note on Hegel, pp. 62–63). Helmuth Plessner, who as the first modern

[25] *Gesammelte Schriften,* 3rd ed. (Berlin: Verlag von B. G. Teubner, 1923), II, 31.
[26] 6th ed. (Halle: Max Niemeyer, 1927).

philosopher in his book *Macht und menschliche Natur* [27] dared to advance a political anthropology of a grand style, correctly says that there exists no philosophy and no anthropology which is not politically relevant, just as there is no philosophically irrelevant politics. He has recognized in particular that philosophy and anthropology, as specifically applicable to the totality of knowledge, cannot, like any specialized discipline, be neutralized against irrational life decisions. Man, for Plessner, is "primarily a being capable of creating distance" who in his essence is undetermined, unfathomable, and remains an "open question." If one bears in mind the anthropological distinction of evil and good and combines Plessner's "remaining open" with his positive reference to danger, Plessner's theory is closer to evil than to goodness. This thesis coincides with the fact that Hegel and Nietzsche too belong on the side of evil, and finally power itself (according to Burckhardt's well-known and by no means unambiguous expression) is also something evil.

———————— • ————————

I have pointed out several times [28] that the antagonism between the so-called authoritarian and anarchist theories can be traced to these formulas. A part of the theories and postulates which presuppose man to be good is liberal. Without being actually anarchist they are polemically directed against the intervention of the state. Ingenuous anarchism reveals that the belief in the natural goodness of man is closely tied to the radical denial of state and government. One follows from the other, and both foment each other. For the liberals, on the other hand, the goodness of man signifies nothing more than an argument with whose aid the state is made to serve society. This means that society determines its own order and that state and government are subordinate and must be distrustingly

[27] (Berlin: Junker & Dünnhaupt, 1931).

[28] *Politische Theologie*, pp. 50 ff.; *Die Diktatur: Von den Anfängen des modernen Souveränitätsgedankens bis zum proletarischen Klassenkampf* (Munich: Duncker & Humblot, 1921, 1928; Berlin, 1964), pp. 9, 109, 112 ff., 123, 148.

controlled and bound to precise limits. The classical formulation by Thomas Paine says: society is the result of our reasonably regulated needs, government is the result of our wickedness.[29] The radicalism vis-à-vis state and government grows in proportion to the radical belief in the goodness of man's nature. Bourgeois liberalism was never radical in a political sense. Yet it remains self-evident that liberalism's negation of state and the political, its neutralizations, depoliticalizations, and declarations of freedom have likewise a certain political meaning, and in a concrete situation these are polemically directed against a specific state and its political power. But this is neither a political theory nor a political idea. Although liberalism has not radically denied the state, it has, on the other hand, neither advanced a positive theory of state nor on its own discovered how to reform the state, but has attempted only to tie the political to the ethical and to subjugate it to economics. It has produced a doctrine of the separation and balance of powers, i.e., a system of checks and controls of state and government. This cannot be characterized as either a theory of state or a basic political principle.

What remains is the remarkable and, for many, certainly disquieting diagnosis that all genuine political theories presuppose man to be evil, i.e., by no means an unproblematic but a dangerous and dynamic being. This can be easily documented in the works of every specific political thinker. Insofar as they reveal themselves as such they all agree on the idea of a problematic human nature, no matter how distinct they are in rank and prominent in history. It suffices here to cite Machiavelli, Hobbes, Bossuet, Fichte (as soon as he forgets his humanitarian idealism), de Maistre, Donoso Cortés, H. Taine, and Hegel, who, to be sure, at times also shows his double face.

[29] See *Die Diktatur*, p. 114. The formulation by Babeuf in the *Tribun du Peuple:* any institution which does not presuppose the people to be good and the officials corruptible . . . (is reprehensible) is not liberal but meant in the sense of the democratic identity of ruler and ruled.

[Schmitt's Note]

Hegel, nevertheless, remains everywhere political in the decisive sense. Those of his writings which concern the actual problems of his time, particularly the highly gifted work of his youth, *Die Verfassung Deutschlands,* are enduring documentations of the philosophical truth that all spirit is present spirit. This remains visible also through the correctness or incorrectness of Hegel's ephemeral position on historical events of his time. The historical spirit does not reside in baroque representations or even in romantic alibis. That is Hegel's *Hic Rhodus* and the genuineness of a philosophy which does not permit the fabrication of intellectual traps under the pretext of apolitical purity and pure nonpolitics. Of a specifically political nature also is his dialectic of concrete thinking. The often quoted sentence of quantity transforming into quality has a thoroughly political meaning. It is an expression of the recognition that from every domain the point of the political is reached and with it a qualitative new intensity of human groupings. The actual application of this sentence refers to the economic domain and becomes virulent in the nineteenth century. The process of such a transformation executes itself continuously in the autonomous, so-called politically neutral economic domain. The hitherto nonpolitical or pure matter of fact now turns political. When it reaches a certain quantity, economic property, for example, becomes obviously social (or more correctly, political) power, *propriété* turns into *pouvoir,* and what is at first only an economically motivated class antagonism turns into a class struggle of hostile groups.

Hegel also offers the first polemically political definition of the bourgeois. The bourgeois is an individual who does not want to leave the apolitical riskless private sphere. He rests in the possession of his private property, and under the justification of his possessive individualism he acts as an individual against the totality. He is a man who finds his compensation for his political nullity in the fruits of freedom and enrichment and above all in the total security of its use. Consequently he wants to be spared bravery and exempted from the danger of a violent death.[30]

Hegel has also advanced a definition of the enemy which in general has been evaded by modern philosophers. The enemy is a negated otherness. But this negation is mutual and this mutuality of negations has its own concrete existence, as a relation between enemies; this relation of two nothingnesses on both sides bears the danger of war. "This war is not a war of families against families, but between peoples, and hatred becomes thereby undifferentiated and freed from all particular personality." *

The question is how long the spirit of Hegel has actually resided in Berlin. In any event, the new political tendency which dominated Prussia after 1840 preferred to avail itself of a conservative philosophy of state, especially one furnished by Friedrich Julius Stahl, whereas Hegel wandered to Moscow via Karl Marx and Lenin. His dialectical method became established there and found its concrete expression in a new concrete-enemy concept, namely that of the international class enemy, and transformed itself, the dialectical method, as well as everything else, legality and illegality, the state, even the compromise with the enemy, into a weapon of this battle. The actuality of Hegel is very much alive in Georg Lukács.[31] He cites an expression by Lenin which Hegel would have made with reference to the political entity of a warring people instead of a class: "Persons, says Lenin, who think of politics as small tricks which at times border on deceit must be decisively refuted. Classes cannot be deceived."

————————— • —————————

The question is not settled by psychological comments on optimism or pessimism. It follows according to the anarchist method

[30] "Wissenschaftliche Behandlungsarten des Naturrechts," *Sämtliche Werke* (Glockner edition; Stuttgart: Frommanns Verlag, 1927), I, 499.

* The translator divided Hegel's intricate phrases which Schmitt quotes. The critical reader may contrive a better translation.

[31] *Geschichte und Klassenbewusstsein* (Berlin: Luchterhand, 1968), *Lenin* (Berlin: Luchterhand, 1968).

that only individuals who consider man to be evil are evil. Those who consider him to be good, namely the anarchists, are then entitled to some sort of superiority or control over the evil ones. The problem thus begins anew. One must pay more attention to how very different the anthropological presuppositions are in the various domains of human thought. With methodological necessity an educator will consider man capable of being educated. A jurist of private law starts with the sentence "one who is presumed to be good." [32] A theologian ceases to be a theologian when he no longer considers man to be sinful or in need of redemption and no longer distinguishes between the chosen and the nonchosen. The moralist presupposes a freedom of choice between good and evil.[33] Because the sphere of the political is in the final analysis determined by the real possibility of enmity, political conceptions and ideas cannot very well start with an anthropological optimism. This would dissolve the possibility of enmity and, thereby, every specific political consequence.

The connection of political theories with theological dogmas of sin which appear prominently in Bossuet, Maistre, Bonald,

[32] The liberal J. K. Bluntschli in his *Lehre vom modernen Staat,* Part III, *Politik als Wissenschaft* (Aalen: Scientia Verlag, 1965, p. 550) asserts against Stahl's doctrine of parties that jurisprudence (which incidentally has nothing to do with this doctrine of parties) does not start from the evilness of man but from the "golden rule of jurists: whoever is presumed to be good," whereas Stahl, in accordance with theology, puts at the top of his thoughts the sinfulness of man. Jurisprudence for Bluntschli is naturally civil law (see above, note 1). The golden rule of jurists derives its meaning from a regulation of the burden of proof. Moreover, it presupposes that a state exists which has created the external conditions of morality by producing a normal situation within which man can be good.

[33] To the extent to which theology becomes moral theology, this freedom-of-choice aspect prevails and weakens the doctrine of the radical evilness of man. "Men are free and endowed with the opportunity to choose [between good and evil]; therefore it is not true that some [men] are good by nature and others evil by nature." Irenaeus, *Contra haereses* (Bk. IV, Ch. 37, Migne, *Patrologia Graeca* VII, col. 1099).

Donoso Cortés, and Friedrich Julius Stahl, among others, is explained by the relationship of these necessary presuppositions. The fundamental theological dogma of the evilness of the world and man leads, just as does the distinction of friend and enemy, to a categorization of men and makes impossible the undifferentiated optimism of a universal conception of man. In a good world among good people, only peace, security, and harmony prevail. Priests and theologians are here just as superfluous as politicians and statesmen. What the denial of original sin means socially and from the viewpoint of individual psychology has been shown by Ernst Troeltsch in his *Soziallehren der christlichen Kirchen und Gruppen* and Seillière (in many publications about romanticism and romantics) in the examples of numerous sects, heretics, romantics, and anarchists. The methodical connection of theological and political presuppositions is clear. But theological interference generally confuses political concepts because it shifts the distinction usually into moral theology. Political thinkers such as Machiavelli, Hobbes, and often Fichte presuppose with their pessimism only the reality or possibility of the distinction of friend and enemy. For Hobbes, truly a powerful and systematic political thinker, the pessimistic conception of man is the elementary presupposition of a specific system of political thought. He also recognized correctly that the conviction of each side that it possesses the truth, the good, and the just bring about the worst enmities, finally the war of all against all. This fact is not the product of a frightful and disquieting fantasy nor of a philosophy based on free competition by a bourgeois society in its first stage (Tönnies), but is the fundamental presupposition of a specific political philosophy.

These political thinkers are always aware of the concrete possibility of an enemy. Their realism can frighten men in need of security. Without wanting to decide the question of the nature of man one may say in general that as long as man is well off or willing to put up with things, he prefers the illusion of an undisturbed calm and does not endure pessimists. The political adversaries of a clear political theory will, therefore, easily refute political phenomena and truths in the name of some autonomous discipline as amoral, uneconomical, unscientific and above all declare this—and this is politically relevant—a devilry worthy of being combated.

[Schmitt's Note]

This misfortune occurred to Machiavelli, who, had he been a Machiavellian, would sooner have written an edifying book than his ill-reputed *Prince*. In actuality, Machiavelli was on the defensive as was also his country, Italy, which in the sixteenth century had been invaded by Germans, Frenchmen, Spaniards, and Turks. At the beginning of the nineteenth century the situation of the ideological defensive was repeated in Germany—during the revolutionary and Napoleonic invasions of the French. When it became important for the German people to defend themselves against an expanding enemy armed with a humanitarian ideology, Machiavelli was rehabilitated by Fichte and Hegel.

———————— • ————————

The worst confusion arises when concepts such as justice and freedom are used to legitimize one's own political ambitions and to disqualify or demoralize the enemy. In the shadow of an embracing political decision and in the security of a stable political state organization, law, whether private or public, has its own relatively independent domain. As with every domain of human endeavor and thought, it can be utilized to support or refute other domains. But it is necessary to pay attention to the political meaning of such utilizations of law and morality, and above all of the word rule or sovereignty of law.

First, law can signify here the existing positive laws and lawgiving methods which should continue to be valid. In this case the rule of law means nothing else than the legitimization of a specific *status quo,* the preservation of which interests particularly those whose political power or economic advantage would stabilize itself in this law. Second, appealing to law can signify that a higher or better law, a so-called natural law or law of reason, is set against the law of the *status quo*. In this case it is clear to a politician that the rule or sovereignty of this type of law signifies the rule and sovereignty of men or groups who can appeal to this higher law and thereby decide its content and how and by whom it should be applied. Hobbes has drawn these simple consequences of political thought without confusion and more clearly than anyone else. He has emphasized time and again that the sovereignty of law means only the sovereignty of men who draw up and administer this law. The rule of a higher order, according to Hobbes, is an empty phrase if it does not signify politically that certain men of this higher order rule over men of a lower order. The independence and completeness of political thought is here irrefutable. There always are concrete human groupings which fight other concrete human groupings in the name of justice, humanity, order, or peace. When being reproached for immorality and cynicism, the spectator of political phenomena can always recognize in such reproaches a political weapon used in actual combat.

Political thought and political instinct prove themselves theoretically and practically in the ability to distinguish friend and enemy. The high points of politics are simultaneously the moments in which the enemy is, in concrete clarity, recognized as the enemy.

[Schmitt's Note]

With regard to modern times, there are many powerful outbreaks of such enmity: there is the by no means harmless *écrasez l'infame* of the eighteenth century; the fanatical hatred of Napoleon felt by the German barons Stein and Kleist ("Exterminate them [the French], the Last Judgment will not ask you for your reasons"); Lenin's annihilating sentences against bourgeois and western capitalism. All these are surpassed by Cromwell's enmity towards papist Spain. He says in his speech of September 17, 1656: "The first thing, therefore, that I shall speak to is *That* that is the first lesson of Nature: Being and Preservation. . . . The conservation of that, 'namely of our National Being,' is first to be viewed with respect to those who seek to undo it, and so make it *not to be.*" Let us thus consider our enemies, "the Enemies to the very Being of these Nations" (he always repeats this "very Being" or "National Being" and then proceeds):. "Why, truly, your great Enemy is the Spaniard. He is a natural enemy. He is naturally so; he is naturally so throughout,—by reason of that enmity that is in him against whatsoever is of God. 'Whatsoever is of God' which is in *you,* or which may be in you." Then he repeats: "The Spaniard is your enemy," his "enmity is put into him by God." He is "the natural enemy, the providential enemy," and he who considers him to be an "accidental enemy" is "not well acquainted with Scripture and the things of God," who says: " 'I will put enmity between your seed and her seed' " (Gen. III: 15). With France one can make peace, not with Spain because it is a papist state, and the pope maintains peace only as long as he wishes.[34]

———————— • ————————

But also vice versa: everywhere in political history, in foreign as well as in domestic politics, the incapacity or the unwillingness to make this distinction is a symptom of the political end. In Russia, before the Revolution, the doomed classes romanticized the Russian peasant as good, brave, and Christian muzhik. A relativistic bourgeoisie in a confused Europe searched all sorts of exotic cultures for the purpose of making them an object of its aesthetic consumption. The aristocratic society in France before the Revolution of 1789 sentimentalized "man who is by nature good" and the virtue of the masses. Tocqueville recounts this situation [35] in words whose shuddering tension arises in him from a specific political pathos: nobody scented the revolution; it is incredible to see the security and un-suspiciousness with which these privileged spoke of the goodness, mildness, and innocence of the people when 1793 was already upon them—*spectacle ridicule et terrible.*

[34] *Oliver Cromwell's Letters and Speeches* (Carlyle edition; New York: E. P. Dutton & Co., 1907), III, pp. 149, 150, 151, 153.

[35] *L'Ancien Régime et la révolution,* p. 228.

8

Liberalism * has changed all political conceptions in a peculiar and systematic fashion. Like any other significant human movement liberalism too, as a historical force, has failed to elude the political. Its neutralizations and depoliticalizations (of education, the economy, etc.) are, to be sure, of political significance. Liberals of all countries have engaged in politics just as other parties and have in the most different ways coalesced with nonliberal elements and ideas. There are national liberals, social liberals, free conservatives, liberal Catholics, and so on.[36] In particular they have tied themselves to very illiberal, essentially political, and even democratic movements leading to the total state.[37] But the question is whether a

---

* This section rests on Schmitt's clear-cut distinction between liberalism and democracy, which he had already developed in 1923 (*Die geistesgeschichtliche Lage des heutigen Parlamentarismus* (Munich: Duncker & Humblot, 1923, 1926; Berlin, 1961, 1969). It is his assertion that liberalism destroys democracy and democracy liberalism.

[36] The combinations could easily be multiplied. German romanticism from 1800 until 1830 is a traditional and feudal liberalism. Sociologically speaking, it is a modern bourgeois movement in which the citizenry was not sufficiently powerful to do away with the then existing political power bathed in feudal tradition. Liberalism therefore wanted to coalesce with tradition as, later on, with the essentially democratic nationalism and socialism. No specific political theory can be derived from consequent bourgeois liberalism. That is the final reason why romanticism cannot possess a political theory but always accommodates itself to contemporaneous political energies.† Historians, such as G. von Below, who always want to see only a conservative romanticism must ignore the palpable historical associations. The three great literary heralds of typical liberal parliamentarianism are typical romantics: Burke, Chateaubriand, and Benjamin Constant.

[37] On the contrast of liberalism and democracy see Carl Schmitt, *Die geistesgeschichtliche Lage,* 2nd ed. (1926), pp. 13 ff.; furthermore, the article

---

† This topic has been exhaustively treated by Schmitt in his *Politische Romantik,* 2nd ed. (Munich: Duncker & Humblot, 1925; Berlin, 1968). See particularly the preface.

specific political idea can be derived from the pure and consequential concept of individualistic liberalism. This is to be denied.

The negation of the political, which is inherent in every consistent individualism, leads necessarily to a political practice of distrust toward all conceivable political forces and forms of state and government, but never produces on its own a positive theory of state, government, and politics. As a result, there exists a liberal policy in the form of a polemical antithesis against state, church, or other institutions which restrict individual freedom. There exists a liberal policy of trade, church, and education, but absolutely no liberal politics, only a liberal critique of politics. The systematic theory of liberalism concerns almost solely the internal struggle against the power of the state. For the purpose of protecting individual freedom and private property, liberalism provides a series of methods for hindering and controlling the state's and government's power. It makes of the state a compromise and of its institutions a ventilating system and, moreover, balances monarchy against democracy and vice versa. In critical times—particularly 1848—this led to such a contradictory position that all good observers, such as Lorenz von Stein, Karl Marx, Friedrich Julius Stahl, Donoso Cortés, despaired of trying to find here a political principle or an intellectually consistent idea.

In a very systematic fashion liberal thought evades or ignores state and politics and moves instead in a typical always recurring polarity of two heterogeneous spheres, namely ethics and economics, intellect and trade, education and property. The critical distrust of state and politics is easily explained by the principles of a system whereby the individual must remain *terminus a quo* and *terminus*

---

by F. Tönnies, "Demokratie und Parlamentarismus," *Schmollers Jahrbuch*, Vol. 51, No. 2 (1927), pp. 1–44. He recognizes the sharp division between liberalism and democracy. See also the very interesting article by H. Hefele, "Demokratie und Liberalismus," *Hochland* I (October 1924), 34–43. On the connection of democracy and the total state see above, pp. 22–25.

ad quem. In case of need, the political entity must demand the sacrifice of life. Such a demand is in no way justifiable by the individualism of liberal thought. No consistent individualism can entrust to someone other than to the individual himself the right to dispose of the physical life of the individual. An individualism in which anyone other than the free individual himself were to decide upon the substance and dimension of his freedom would be only an empty phrase. For the individual as such there is no enemy with whom he must enter into a life-and-death struggle if he personally does not want to do so. To compel him to fight against his will is, from the viewpoint of the private individual, lack of freedom and repression. All liberal pathos turns against repression and lack of freedom. Every encroachment, every threat to individual freedom and private property and free competition is called repression and is *eo ipso* something evil. What this liberalism still admits of state, government, and politics is confined to securing the conditions for liberty and eliminating infringements on freedom.

We thus arrive at an entire system of demilitarized and depoliticized concepts. A few may here be enumerated in order to show the incredibly coherent systematics of liberal thought, which, despite all reversals, has still not been replaced in Europe today [1932]. These liberal concepts typically move between ethics (intellectuality) and economics (trade). From this polarity they attempt to annihilate the political as a domain of conquering power and repression. The concept of private law serves as a lever and the notion of private property forms the center of the globe, whose poles—ethics and economics—are only the contrasting emissions from this central point.

Ethical or moral pathos and materialist economic reality combine in every typical liberal manifestation and give every political concept a double face. Thus the political concept of battle in liberal thought becomes competition in the domain of economics and discussion in the intellectual realm. Instead of a clear distinction between the two different states, that of war and that of peace, there appears the dynamic of perpetual competition and perpetual discussion. The state turns into society: on the ethical-intellectual side into an ideological humanitarian conception of humanity, and on the other into an economic-technical system of production and traffic. The self-understood will to repel the enemy in a given battle situation turns into a rationally constructed social ideal or program, a tendency or an economic calculation. A politically united people becomes, on the one hand, a culturally interested public, and, on the other, partially an industrial concern and its employers, partially a mass of consumers. At the intellectual pole, government and power turns into propaganda and mass manipulation, and at the economic pole, control.

These dissolutions aim with great precision at subjugating state and politics, partially into an individualistic domain of private law and morality, partially into economic notions. In doing so they deprive state and politics of their specific meaning. Outside of the political, liberalism not only recognizes with self-evident logic the autonomy of different human realms but drives them toward specialization and even toward complete isolation. That art is a daughter of freedom, that aesthetic value judgment is absolutely autonomous, that artistic genius is sovereign—all this is axiomatic of liberalism. In some countries a genuine liberal pathos came to the fore only when this autonomous freedom of art was endangered by moralistic apostles of tradition. Morality became autonomous vis-à-vis metaphysics and religion, science vis-à-vis religion, art, and morality, etc. The most important example of such an autonomy is the validity of norms and laws of economics. That production and consumption, price formation and market have their own sphere and can be directed neither by ethics nor aesthetics, nor by religion, nor, least of all, by politics was considered one of the few truly unquestionable dogmas of this liberal age. With great passion political viewpoints were deprived of every validity and subjugated to the norms and orders of morality, law, and economics. In the concrete reality of the political, no abstract orders or norms but always real human groupings and associations rule over the other human groupings and associations. Politically, the rule of morality, law, and economics always assumes a concrete political meaning.

[Schmitt's Note]

Note (unchanged from the year 1927): The ideological structure of the Peace of Versailles corresponds precisely to this polarity of ethical pathos and economic calculation. Article 231 forces the German Reich to recognize its responsibility for all war damages and losses. This establishes a foundation for a juridic and moral value judgment. Avoided are such political concepts as annexation. The cession of Alsace-Lorraine is a *désannexion*, in other words a restitution of an injustice. The cession of Polish and Danish territories serves the ideal claim of the nationality principle. The seizure of the colonies is even proclaimed (Article 22) to be an act of selfless humanity. The economic counterpole of this idealism is reparations, i.e., a continuous and unlimited economic exploitation of the vanquished. The result is that such a treaty could not realize a political concept such as freedom, and therefore it became necessary to initiate new "true" peace treaties: the London Protocol of August 1924 (Dawes Plan), Locarno of October 1925, entry into the League of Nations in September 1926—the series is not at an end yet.

———————— • ————————

The word repression is utilized in liberal theory as a reproach against state and politics. This would have been nothing more than a powerless curse word of political debate if it had not been integrated into a large metaphysical and historical system. It gained thereby a broader horizon and a stronger moral conviction. The enlightened eighteenth century believed in a clear and simple upward line of human progress. Progress should above all result in the intellectual and moral perfection of humanity. The line moved between two points: from religious fanaticism to intellectual liberty, from dogma to criticism, from superstition to enlightenment, from darkness to light. In the first half of the nineteenth century, two symptomatic triple-structured constructions appear: Hegel's dialectical succession (family—civil society—state) and Comte's three stages (from theology via metaphysics to positive science). The triple structure weakens the polemical punch of the double-structured antithesis. Therefore, soon after a period of order, exhaustion, and attempts at restoration, when the battle began again, the simple double-structured antithesis prevailed immediately. Even in Germany, where it was not meant to be warlike, Hegel's triple-structured scheme was pushed aside in the second part of the nineteenth century in favor of the dual one, domination and association (in Gierke), or community and society (in Tönnies).

The most conspicuous and historically the most effective example is the antithesis formulated by Karl Marx: bourgeoisie and proletariat. This antithesis concentrates all antagonisms of world history into one single final battle against the last enemy of humanity. It does so by integrating the many bourgeois parties on earth into a single order, on the one hand, and likewise the proletariat, on the other. By so doing a mighty friend-enemy grouping is forged. Its power of conviction during the nineteenth century resided above all in the fact that it followed its liberal bourgeois enemy into its own domain, the economic, and challenged it, so to speak, in its home territory with its own weapons. This was necessary because the turning toward economics was decided by the victory of industrial society. The year of this victory, 1814, was the year in which England had triumphed over the military imperialism of Napoleon. The most simple and transparent theory of this historical development is advanced by H. Spencer. He sees human history as a development from the military-feudal to the industrial-commercial society. But the first already systematic expression, the treatise *De l'esprit de conquête,* had been published in 1814 by Benjamin Constant, the initiator of the whole liberal spirit of the nineteenth century.

In the eighteenth century the idea of progress was primarily humanitarian-moral and intellectual, it was a spiritual progress; in the nineteenth it became economic-industrial-technological. This mutation is decisive. It was believed that the economy is the vehicle of this very complex development. Economy, trade and industry, technological perfection, freedom, and rationalization were considered allies. Despite its offensive thrust against feudalism, reaction, and the police state, it was judged as essentially peaceful, in contrast to warlike force and repression. The characteristic nineteenth-century scheme is thereby formed:

Freedom, progress and reason	against	feudalism, reaction and force
in alliance with		in alliance with
economy, industry and technology	against	state, war and politics
as		as
parliamentarianism	against	dictatorship.

The complete inventory of this system of antitheses and their possible combinations is contained in the 1814 treatise by Benjamin Constant. He maintains that we are in an age which must necessarily replace the age of wars, just as the age of wars had necessarily to precede it. Then follows the characterization of both ages: the one aims at winning the goods of life by peaceful exchange (*obtenir de gré à gré*), the other by war and repression. This is the *impulsion sauvage,* the other, on the contrary, *le calcul civilisé.* Since war and conquest are not procuring amenities and comforts, wars are thereby no longer useful, and the victorious war is also bad business for the victor. Moreover, the enormous development of modern war technology (Constant cites particularly the artillery upon which the technological superiority of the Napoleonic armies rested primarily) made senseless everything which had previously been considered in war heroic, glorious, personal courage, and delight in fighting. According to Constant's conclusion, war has lost every usefulness as well as every attraction; *l'homme n'est plus entraîné à s'y livrer, ni par intérêt, ni par passion.* In the past, the warring nations had sub-jugated the trading peoples; today it is the other way round.

The extraordinarily intricate coalition of economy, freedom, technology, ethics, and parliamentarianism has long ago finished off its old enemy: the residues of the absolute state and a feudal aristocracy; and with the disappearance of the enemy it has lost its original meaning. Now new groupings and coalitions appear. Economy is no longer *eo ipso* freedom; technology does not serve comforts only, but just as much the production of dangerous weapons and instruments. Progress no longer produces *eo ipso* the humanitarian and moral perfection which was considered progress in the eighteenth century. A technological rationalization can be the opposite of an economic rationalization. Nevertheless, Europe's spiritual atmosphere continues to remain until this very day under the spell of this nineteenth-century historical interpretation. Until recently its formulas and concepts retained a force which appeared to survive the death of its old adversary.

[Schmitt's Note]

The best example of this polarity of state and society is con-tained in the theses of Franz Oppenheimer. He declares his aim to be the destruction of the state. His liberalism is so radical that he no longer permits the state to be even an armed office guard. The de-struction is effected by advancing a value- and passion-ridden definition. The concept of state should be determined by political means, the concept of society (in essence nonpolitical) by economic means. But the qualifications by which political and economic means are then defined are nothing more than typical expressions of that pathos against politics and state. They swing in the polarity of ethics and economics and unveil polemical antitheses in which is mirrored the nineteenth-century German polemical tension of state and society, politics and economy. The economic way is declared to be reciprocity of production and consumption, therefore mutuality,

equality, justice, and freedom, and finally nothing less than the
spiritual union of fellowship, brotherliness, and justice.[38] The political way appears on the other hand as a conquering power outside
the domain of economics, namely, thievery, conquest, and crimes of
all sorts. A hierarchical value system of the relation of state and
society is maintained. But whereas Hegel's systematized conception
of the German state in the nineteenth century considered it to be a
realm of morality and objective reason high above the appetitive
domain of egoistic society, the value judgment is now turned around.
Society as a sphere of peaceful justice now stands infinitely higher
than the state, which is degraded to a region of brutal immorality.
The roles are changed, the apotheosis remains.

But this in actuality is not permissible and neither moral nor
psychological, least of all scientific, to simply define by moral dis-
qualifications, by confronting the good, the just, and the peaceful
with filthy, evil, rapacious, and criminal politics. With such methods
one could just as well the other way around define politics as the
sphere of honest rivalry and economics as a world of deception. The
connection of politics with thievery, force, and repression is, in the
final analysis, no more precise than is the connection of economics
with cunning and deception. Exchange and deception are often not
far apart. A domination of men based upon pure economics must
appear a terrible deception if, by remaining nonpolitical, it thereby
evades political responsibility and visibility. Exchange by no means
precludes the possibility that one of the contractors experiences a
disadvantage and that a system of mutual contracts finally de-
teriorates into a system of the worst exploitation and repression.
When the exploited and the repressed attempt to defend themselves
in such a situation, they cannot do so by economic means. Evidently,
the possessor of economic power would consider every attempt to
change its power position by extra-economic means as violence and

[38] See the compilation by Fritz Sander, "Gesellschaft und Staat, Studie
zur Gesellschaftslehre von Franz Oppenheimer," *Archiv für Sozialwissenschaft,* 56 (1926), 384–385.

crime, and will seek methods to hinder this. That ideal construction of a society based on exchange and mutual contracts and, *eo ipso,* peaceful and just is thereby eliminated. Unfortunately, also, usurers and extortioners appeal to the inviolability of contracts and to the sentence *pacta sunt servanda.* The domain of exchange has its narrow limits and its specific categories, and not all things possess an exchange value. No matter how large the financial bribe may be, there is no money equivalent for political freedom and political independence.

———————— • ————————

State and politics cannot be exterminated. The world will not become depoliticalized with the aid of definitions and constructions, all of which circle the polarity of ethics and economics. Economic antagonisms can become political, and the fact that an economic power position could arise proves that the point of the political may be reached from the economic as well as from any other domain. The often quoted phrase by Walter Rathenau, namely that the destiny today is not politics but economics, originated in this context. It would be more exact to say that politics continues to remain the destiny, but what has occurred is that economics has become political and thereby the destiny.

It is also erroneous to believe that a political position founded on economic superiority is "essentially unwarlike," as Joseph Schumpeter says in his *Zur Soziologie der Imperialismen.*[39] Essentially unwarlike is the terminology based on the essence of liberal ideology. An imperialism based on pure economic power will naturally attempt to sustain a worldwide condition which enables it to apply and manage, unmolested, its economic means, e.g., terminating credit, embargoing raw materials, destroying the currencies of others, and so on. Every attempt of a people to withdraw itself from the effects of such "peaceful" methods is considered by this imperialism as extra-economic power. Pure economic imperialism will also apply

[39] (Tübingen: J. C. Mohr [Paul Siebeck], 1919).

a stronger, but still economic, and therefore (according to this terminology) nonpolitical, essentially peaceful means of force. A 1921 League of Nations resolution [40] enumerates as examples: economic sanctions and severance of the food supply from the civilian population. Finally, it has sufficient technical means to brings about violent death. Modern means of annihilation have been produced by enormous investments of capital and intelligence, surely to be used if necessary.

For the application of such means, a new and essentially pacifist vocabulary has been created. War is condemned but executions, sanctions, punitive expeditions, pacifications, protection of treaties, international police, and measures to assure peace remain. The adversary is thus no longer called an enemy but a disturber of peace and is thereby designated to be an outlaw of humanity. A war waged to protect or expand economic power must, with the aid of propaganda, turn into a crusade and into the last war of humanity. This is implicit in the polarity of ethics and economics, a polarity astonishingly systematic and consistent. But this allegedly nonpolitical and apparently even antipolitical system serves existing or newly emerging friend-and-enemy groupings and cannot escape the logic of the political.

[40] Number 14 of the second gathering, "guidelines" to carrying out Article 16 of the Covenant.

NOTES ON CARL SCHMITT,
THE CONCEPT OF THE POLITICAL

By Leo Strauss
Translated by J. Harvey Lomax

I

[1]   The treatise by Schmitt[1] serves the question of the "order of the human things" (95), that is, the question of the state. In view of the fact that in the present age the state has become more questionable than it has been for centuries or more (23 f.), understanding the state requires a radical foundation, "a simple and elementary presentation" of what the basis of the state is, which means the basis of the political; for "the concept of the state presupposes the concept of the political" (20).

[2]   This thesis, with which the investigation of the concept of the political is begun, must be understood in accordance with Schmitt's own general principles of understanding. Following these principles, the sentence "the political precedes the state" can manifest the desire to express not an eternal truth but only a present truth. For "all spirit [is] only spirit of the present" (79); "all concepts of the spiritual sphere, including the concept of spirit, are in themselves pluralistic and are to be understood only in terms of their concrete political existence" (84); "all political concepts, ideas, and words [have] a polemical meaning; they have a concrete opposition in view, they are tied to a concrete situation . . ." (31). In accordance with these principles, it must be asked: To what extent does the present situation compel us to recognize that the basis of the state is the political? Against what opponent does the political emerge as the basis of the state?

[3]   The present situation is characterized by the fact that a process three hundred years old has "reached its end" (94). The age at the end of which we find ourselves is "the age of neutraliza-

---

[1] *Der Begriff des Politischen. Mit einer Rede über das Zeitalter der Neutralisierungen und Entpolitisierungen neu herausgegeben von Carl Schmitt* (Munich and Leipzig, 1932). The parenthetical page numbers identify page numbers of that text. [Those numbers have been replaced in this translation by the page numbers of the 1963 edition.—Heinrich Meier]

tions and depoliticizations." Depoliticization not only is the accidental or even necessary result of the modern development but is
its original and authentic goal; the movement in which the modern
spirit has gained its greatest efficacy, liberalism, is characterized
precisely by the *negation* of the political (68 ff.). If liberalism has
already become implausible, if it accordingly must be countered
by "another system," then the first word against liberalism must
in any case be: the *position* of the political. And if liberalism believed that by means of its negation of the political it could bring
about the foundation of the state or, more accurately, the establishment of rational social relations, after the failure of liberalism one
cannot help thinking that the state can be understood only from
the position of the political. Thus Schmitt's basic thesis is entirely
dependent upon the polemic against liberalism; it is to be understood only qua polemical, only "in terms of concrete political existence."

[4] Schmitt's task is determined by the fact that liberalism
has failed. The circumstances of this failure are as follows: Liberalism negated the political; yet liberalism has not thereby eliminated
the political from the face of the earth but only has hidden it;
liberalism has led to politics' being engaged in by means of an
antipolitical mode of discourse. Liberalism has thus killed not the
political but only understanding of the political, sincerity regarding
the political (65 ff.). In order to remove the smokescreen over
reality that liberalism produces, the political must be made apparent as such and as simply undeniable. The political must first be
brought out of the concealment into which liberalism has cast it,
so that the question of the state can be seriously put.

[5] It is thus insufficient to establish as a fact that liberalism
has failed, to show how liberalism drives itself ad absurdum in
every political action, to indicate "that all good observers . . .
despaired of finding here [in liberalism] any political principle or
intellectual consistency" (69). Nor does it suffice to attain the insight that the manifest inconsistency of all liberal politics is the

necessary consequence of the fundamental negation of the political
(69). What is needed rather is to replace the "astonishingly consistent systematics of liberal *thought*," which is manifest within the
inconsistency of liberal *politics,* by "another system" (70), namely,
a system that does not negate the political but brings it into recognition.

[6]   Schmitt is aware that the "astonishingly consistent . . .
systematics of liberal thought" has, "despite all setbacks, still not been
replaced in Europe today by any other system" (70), and this awareness alone suffices to characterize the significance of his efforts; for
with this awareness he stands wholly alone among the opponents of
liberalism, who usually carry an elaborate unliberal doctrine in their
pocket. In making this observation Schmitt points to the basic diffi-
culty of his own investigation also. For if it is true that the "systematics of liberal thought" has "still not been replaced in Europe today
by any other system," it is to be expected that he, too, will be compelled to make use of elements of liberal thought in the presentation
of his views. The tentativeness of Schmitt's statements results from
that compulsion. Schmitt himself explicitly says so: he wants to do
no more than "'to delimit' theoretically an immense problem"; the
theses of his text "are conceived as a *point of departure* for an objective
discussion" (96). The foregoing engenders the critic's duty to pay
more attention to what distinguishes Schmitt from the prevailing
view than to the respects in which he merely follows the prevailing
view.

II

[7]   Schmitt expressly desists from providing an "exhaustive
definition" of the political (26). From the outset he understands
the question of the "*essence* of the political" (20) as the question of
what is specific to the political (21 and 26 f.). He does so, to be sure,
not because he regards the question of the genus (within which
the specific difference of the political has to be stipulated) as already

answered or even as immaterial, but precisely because of his deep
suspicion of what is today the most obvious answer: he pioneers a
path to an original answer to the genus question by using the
phenomenon of the political to push the most obvious answer ad
absurdum. What is still today, despite all challenges, the most
obvious, genuinely liberal answer to the question of the genus
within which the peculiarity of the political and, therewith, of the
state is to be defined is that genus is the *"culture,"* that is, the
totality of "human thought and action," which is divided into
"various, relatively independent domains" (26), into "provinces of
culture" (Natorp). Schmitt would remain within the horizon of
this answer if, as at first appears, he were to say: just as "in the
domain of the moral the ultimate distinctions are good and evil,
in the aesthetic domain beautiful and ugly, in the economic domain
useful and harmful," so the "specifically political distinction . . . is
the distinction between friend and enemy" (26). However, this
ordering of the political next to, and equivalent to, the other "provinces of culture" is expressly rejected: the distinction between
friend and enemy is *"not equivalent and analogous* . . . to those
other distinctions"; the political does *not* describe "a new *domain
of its own"* (27). What is hereby said is that the understanding of
the political implies a fundamental critique of at least the prevailing concept of culture.

[8] Schmitt does not express this critique everywhere. He
too, using the terminology of a whole literature, occasionally speaks
of the "various, relatively independent domains of human thought
and action" (26) or of the various "spheres of human life and
thought" (66). In one passage (71) he expresses himself in such a
way that a superficial reader could get the following impression:
after liberalism has brought the autonomy of the aesthetic, of morals, of science, of the economy, etc. into recognition, Schmitt now
seeks, for his part, to bring the autonomy of the political into
recognition, in opposition to liberalism but nonetheless in continuation of liberal aspirations for autonomy. To be sure, the quotation

marks that he places around the word "autonomy" in the expression "autonomy of the various domains of human life" already show how little the foregoing is Schmitt's opinion. This [indication] becomes clearer when he emphasizes the *"matter-of-factness"* with which liberalism "not only recognizes the 'autonomy' of the various domains of human life but exaggerates it to the point of specialization and even to complete isolation" (71). Schmitt's aloofness from the prevailing concept of culture becomes fully clear in the following indirect characterization of the aesthetic: "the path from the metaphysical and the moral to the economic traverses the aesthetic, and the path across aesthetic consumption and enjoyment, be they ever so sublime, is the surest and most comfortable path to the universal economization of spiritual life . . ." (83); for the prevailing concept of culture surely includes recognition of the autonomous value of the aesthetic—assuming that this concept is not altogether constituted precisely by that recognition. This observation leads at least to the demand that the prevailing concept of culture be replaced by another concept of culture. And that replacement will have to be based on the insight into what is specific to the political.

[9] Schmitt expressly forgoes, as we have seen, an "exhaustive definition" of the political. Proceeding on the assumption that the "various, relatively independent domains of human thought and action" (the moral, the aesthetic, the economic, etc.) have "their own criteria" by which they are constituted in their relative independence, he asks about the "criterion of the political." The criteria in question have the character of "ultimate distinctions," or, more accurately, of ultimate "oppositions." Thus the criterion of the moral is the opposition of good and evil, the criterion of the aesthetic, the opposition of beautiful and ugly, etc. In taking his bearings by this general relationship, Schmitt defines "the distinction between friend and enemy" as "the specifically political distinction" (26 f.). Here "enemy"—and thus also "friend"—is always to be understood only as the *public* enemy (friend), "a *totality* of men that fights at least potentially, that is, has a real possibility of

fighting, and stands in opposition to a corresponding totality" (29). Of the two elements of the friend-enemy mode of viewing things, the "enemy" element manifestly takes precedence, as is already shown by the fact that when Schmitt explains this viewpoint in detail, he actually speaks only of the meaning of "enemy" (cf. 27, 29, and 32 f.). One may say: every "totality of men" looks around for friends only—it *has* friends only—because it already has enemies; "the essence of political relationships [is] contained in reference to a concrete *opposition*" (30). "Enemy" therefore takes precedence over "friend," because "the potential for a fight that exists in the region of the real" belongs "to the concept of the enemy"—and not already to the concept of the friend as such (33), and "man's life" gains "its specifically *political* tension" from the potential for war, from the "dire emergency," from the "most extreme possibility" (35). But the possibility of war does not merely constitute the political as such; war is not merely "the most extreme political measure"; war is the dire emergency not merely within an "autonomous" region—the region of the political—but for man simply, because war has and retains a "relationship to the real possibility of *physical killing*" (33); this orientation, which is constitutive for the political, shows that the political is *fundamental* and not a "relatively independent domain" alongside others. The political is the "authoritative" (39). It is in this sense that we are to understand the remark that the political is "not equivalent and analogous" to the moral, the aesthetic, the economic, etc. (26).

[10]   This definition of the political has the closest connection to Schmitt's suggested critique of the prevailing concept of culture. This critique questions the "autonomy" of the various "domains of human thought and action." Following the prevailing concept of culture, however, not only are the individual "provinces of culture" "autonomous" in relation to one another, but, prior to them, culture as a whole is already "autonomous," the sovereign creation, the "pure product" of the human spirit. This viewpoint makes us forget that "culture" always presupposes something that

is cultivated: culture is always the *culture of nature.* This expression means, primarily, that culture develops the natural predisposition; it is careful nurture of nature—whether of the soil or of the human spirit makes no difference; it thus *obeys* the orders that nature itself gives. But the statement can also mean *conquering* nature through obedience to nature (*parendo vincere,* in Bacon's phrase); then culture is not so much faithful nurture of nature as a harsh and cunning fight *against* nature. Whether culture is understood as nurture of nature or as a fight with nature depends on how nature is understood: as exemplary order or as disorder to be eliminated. But however culture is understood, "culture" is certainly the culture of nature. "Culture" is to such an extent the culture of nature that culture can be understood as a sovereign creation of the spirit only if the nature being cultivated has been presupposed to be the *opposite* of spirit, and been *forgotten.* Because we now understand by "culture" primarily the culture of *human* nature, the presupposition of culture is primarily human nature; and because man is by his nature an *animal sociale,* the human nature on which culture is based is the natural social relations of men, that is, the way in which man, prior to all culture, behaves toward other men. The term for natural social relations understood in this manner is *status naturalis.* One can therefore say: the foundation of culture is the *status naturalis.*

[11]   *Hobbes* understood the *status civilis* in the sense of the specifically modern concept of culture—here let it remain an open question whether, strictly speaking, there is any concept of culture other than the *modern* one—as the *opposite* of the *status naturalis;* the *status civilis* is the presupposition of every culture in the narrow sense (i.e. every nurture of the arts and sciences) and is itself already based on a particular culture, namely, on a disciplining of the human will. We will here disregard Hobbes's view of the relationship between *status naturalis* and culture (in the broadest sense) as an opposition; here we only emphasize the fact that Hobbes describes the *status naturalis* as the *status belli,* simply, although it

must be borne in mind that "the nature of war, consisteth *not in actual fighting;* but in the known *disposition* thereto" (*Leviathan* XIII). In Schmitt's terminology this statement means that the *status naturalis* is the genuinely *political* status; for, also according to Schmitt, "the political" is found *"not in fighting itself . . .* but in a behavior that is determined by this real *possibility"* (37). It follows that the political that Schmitt brings to bear as fundamental is the "state of nature" that underlies every culture; Schmitt restores the Hobbesian concept of the state of nature to a place of honor (see 59). Therewith the question about the genus within which the specific difference of the political is to be stipulated has also been answered: the political is a *status* of man; indeed, the political is *the* status as the "natural," the fundamental and extreme, status of man.

[12]   To be sure, the state of nature is defined by Schmitt in a fundamentally different fashion than it is by Hobbes. For Hobbes, it is the state of war of individuals; for Schmitt, it is the state of war of groups (especially of nations). For Hobbes, in the state of nature everyone is the enemy of everyone else; for Schmitt, all political behavior is oriented toward *friend* and enemy. This difference has its basis in the *polemical* intention of Hobbes's definition of the state of nature: for the fact that the state of nature is the state of war of all against all is supposed to motivate the abandonment of the state of nature. To this negation of the state of nature or of the political, Schmitt opposes the position of the political.

[13]   Granted, in Hobbes there is no question of a total negation of the political; according to his doctrine, the state of nature continues at least in the relationship between the nations. And thus Hobbes's polemic against the state of nature as the state of war of *individuals*—which Schmitt implicitly adopts, as shown by his comment, expressly following Hobbes, on the relationship between protection and obedience (53; cf. also 46 f.)—does not need to question the political in Schmitt's sense, that is, the "natu-

ral" character of the relationships of human *groups*. Nevertheless, according to Schmitt it belongs to the essence of the political group that it can "demand . . . from the members of its own nation *the readiness to die*" (46); and the justification of this claim is at least qualified by Hobbes: in battle he who deserts the ranks out of fear for his life acts "only" dishonorably, but not unjustly (*Lev.* XXI). The state can justifiably demand from the individual only *conditional* obedience, namely an obedience that does not stand in contradiction to the salvation or preservation of the life of this individual; for the securing of life is the ultimate basis of the state. Therefore, while man is otherwise obliged to unconditional obedience, he is under no obligation to risk his life; for death is the greatest evil. Hobbes does not shrink from the consequence and expressly denies the status of courage as a virtue (*De homine* XIII 9). The same attitude is disclosed in his definition of the *salus populi*: the *salus populi* consists (1) in defense against the enemy from without; (2) in preservation of peace within; (3) in just and modest enrichment of the individual, which is much more readily attained through work and frugality than through victorious wars, and is particularly promoted by the nurture of mechanics and mathematics; (4) in the enjoyment of innocuous freedom (*De cive* XIII 6 and 14). As soon as "humanity" becomes the subject or object of planning, these principles have to lead to the ideal of civilization, that is, to the demand for rational social relations of humanity as *one* "partnership in consumption and production" (58). Hobbes, to a much higher degree than Bacon, for example, is the author of the ideal of civilization. By this very fact he is the founder of liberalism. The right to the securing of life pure and simple—and this right sums up Hobbes's natural right—has fully the character of an inalienable human right, that is, of an individual's *claim* that takes precedence over the state and determines its purpose and its limits; Hobbes's foundation for the natural-right claim to the securing of life pure and simple sets the path to the whole system of human rights in the sense of liberalism, if his foundation does not actually make such a course necessary. Hobbes differs from developed liberalism only, but certainly, by his knowing and seeing *against what* the liberal ideal of civilization has to be persistently fought for: not merely against rotten institutions, against the evil will of a ruling class, but against the natural evil of man; in an unliberal world Hobbes forges ahead to lay the foundation of liberalism against the—*sit venia verbo*—unliberal nature of man, whereas later men, ignorant of their premises and goals, trust in the original goodness (based on God's creation and providence) of human nature or, on the basis of natural-scientific neutrality, nurse hopes for an improvement of nature, hopes unjustified by man's experience of himself. Hobbes, *in view of* the state of nature, attempts to overcome the state of nature within the limits in which it allows of being overcome, whereas later men either dream up a state of nature or, on the basis of a supposed deeper insight into history and therewith into the essence of man, forget the state of nature. But—in all fairness to later men— ultimately that dreaming and that oblivion are merely the consequence of the negation of the state of nature, merely the consequence of the position of civilization introduced by Hobbes.

[14]   If it is true that the final self-awareness of liberalism is the philosophy of culture, we may say in summary that liberalism, sheltered by and engrossed in a world of culture, forgets the foundation of culture, the state of nature, that is, human nature in its dangerousness and endangeredness. Schmitt returns, contrary to liberalism, to its author, Hobbes, in order to strike at the root of liberalism in Hobbes's express negation of the state of nature.[2] Whereas Hobbes in an unliberal world accomplishes the founding

---

[2] In the first edition of this treatise Schmitt had described Hobbes as "by far the greatest and perhaps the sole truly systematic political thinker" (*Archiv für Sozialwissenschaft und Sozialpolitik*, vol. 58, p. 25). Schmitt now speaks of Hobbes only as "a great and truly systematic political thinker" (64). In truth Hobbes is *the* antipolitical thinker ("political" understood in Schmitt's sense).

of liberalism, Schmitt in a liberal world undertakes the critique of liberalism.

III

[15] Schmitt confronts the liberal negation of the political with the position of the political, that is, with the recognition of the reality of the political. For the position of the political it is immaterial, in Schmitt's express opinion, whether one regards the political as desirable or detestable: the intent of the position "is neither bellicose or militarist, nor imperialist, nor pacifist" (33). Schmitt desires only to know *what is*. This statement does not mean that he considers his expositions "value-free," that he wants (whether out of concern for the scientific character of his study or for the freedom of personal decision) to leave open all possibilities for taking an evaluative stance toward the political. Rather, he intends precisely to seal off all such possibilities: the political *cannot* be evaluated at all, cannot be measured by an ideal; applied to the political, *all* ideals are nothing but "abstractions," *all* "normative prescriptions" nothing but "fictions" (49 f. and 28 f.). For the political is constituted by reference "to the real possibility of physical killing" of men by men (33); and "there is no rational purpose, no norm however correct, no program however exemplary, no social ideal however beautiful, no legitimacy or legality that can justify men's killing one another for its own sake" (49 f.).

[16] The position of the political results in the *unpolemical* description of the political. As such, the position opposes Hobbes's polemical description of the state of nature. Hobbes had presented the state of nature as in itself impossible: the state of nature is the state of war of all against all; in the state of nature, everyone is the enemy of everyone else. According to Schmitt, the subjects of the state of nature are not individuals but totalities; furthermore, not every totality is the enemy of every other totality, but alongside

the possibility of enmity the possibilities of alliance and neutrality also exist (35). The state of nature so understood is in itself *possible.* That it is *real,* however, is proved by the whole history of humanity up to the present day. It may be that there will someday be a completely depoliticized state of humanity—"whether and when this state of the earth and of humanity will occur, I do not know"; at any rate that state "for the time being does not exist," and therefore it would be "a dishonest fiction to assume that it is at hand" (54).

[17] Now one cannot—least of all can Schmitt himself—take relief in the fact that the depoliticized state *"for the time being does not exist"* (54), that "war as a real possibility is *still* present *today"* (37). In view of the fact that there is today a powerful movement striving for the total elimination of the real possibility of war and hence the abolition of the political, in view of the fact that this movement not only exercises a great influence upon the mentality of the age but also authoritatively determines the real circumstances—this movement led, after all, to war's being *"today . . .* probably neither something pious, nor something morally good, nor something profitable" (36), whereas in earlier centuries war could indeed be all these things—in view of this fact one must look beyond today and ask: granted that "war as a real possibility is still present today," will war still be a possibility present tomorrow? or the day after tomorrow? In other words: though the abolition of the political may in no way have succeeded *so far,* is not this abolition nevertheless possible in the future? is it not possible at all?

[18] Schmitt gives the following answer to this question: The political is a basic characteristic of human life; politics in this sense *is* destiny; therefore man cannot escape politics (36 f., 66 f., 76 ff.). The inescapability of the political is displayed in the contradiction in which man necessarily becomes entangled if he attempts to eliminate the political. This effort has a prospect of success if and only if it becomes political; that is, if it "is strong

enough to group men into friends and enemies," if it thus "would be able to drive the pacifists into *war* against the nonpacifists, into a 'war against war.'" The war against war will then be undertaken as "the definitively final war of humanity." Such a war, however, is "necessarily especially intensive and inhuman" because in it the enemy is fought as "an inhuman monster . . . that must be not only fended off but definitively annihilated" (37). But humanity cannot be expected to be especially humane and, therefore, unpolitical after having just put behind it an especially inhumane war. Thus the effort to abolish the political for the sake of humanity has as its necessary consequence nothing other than the increase of inhumanity. When it is said that the political is a basic characteristic of human life, in other words that man ceases to be man if he ceases to be political, this statement also, and precisely, means that man ceases to be human when he ceases to be political. If man thus gets entangled in contradictions when he attempts to eliminate the political, that attempt is ultimately possible only through dishonesty: "To curse war as the murder of men, and then to demand of men that—so that there will 'never again be war'—they wage war and kill and allow themselves to be killed in war, is a manifest fraud" (49).

[19] The political is thus not only possible but also real; and not only real but also necessary. It is necessary because it is given in human nature. Therefore the opposition between the negation and the position of the political can be traced back to a quarrel over human nature. The ultimate controversy is whether man is by nature good or evil. Here, however, "good" and "evil" are "not to be taken in a specifically moral or ethical sense"; rather, "good" is to be understood as "undangerous," and "evil" as "dangerous." Thus the ultimate question is "whether man is a dangerous or an undangerous being, a perilous or a harmless, nonperilous being" (59). "All genuine political theories" presuppose man's dangerousness (61). Accordingly, the thesis of man's dangerousness is the ultimate presupposition of the position of the political.

[20] The train of thought just recounted is in all probability not Schmitt's last word, and it is certainly not the most profound thing that he has to say. It conceals a reflection that moves in an entirely different direction, a reflection that cannot be reconciled with the line of thought described above.

[21] Schmitt describes the thesis of the dangerousness of man as the ultimate presupposition of the position of the political: the necessity of the political is as certain as man's dangerousness. But is man's dangerousness unshakably certain? Schmitt himself qualifies the thesis of man's dangerousness as a *"supposition,"* as an "anthropological confession of *faith"* (58). But if man's dangerousness is only supposed or believed in, not genuinely known, the opposite, too, can be regarded as possible, and the attempt to eliminate man's dangerousness (which until now has always really existed) can be put into practice. If man's dangerousness is only believed in, it is in principle *threatened,* and therewith the political is threatened also.

[22] Schmitt concedes that the political is in principle threatened when he says: "Whether and when this [completely apolitical] state of the earth and of humanity will occur, *I do not know"* (54). Now the political could not be threatened if, as Schmitt asserts in a series of passages, it were simply inescapable. One must therefore add an obvious qualifier to his assertion that the political is inescapable, and must understand that assertion as follows: the political is inescapable as long as there is just *one* political opposition, even just as a possibility. Schmitt implies this qualifier in the course of the previously adduced argument against pacifism, for that line of argument presupposes that the opposition between pacifists and nonpacifists does not disappear. The inescapability of the political thus exists only conditionally; ultimately, the political remains threatened.

[23] If the political is ultimately threatened, the position of the political must ultimately be *more* than the recognition of the reality of the political, namely, an espousal of the threatened politi-

cal, an *affirmation* of the political. It is therefore necessary to ask: why does Schmitt affirm the political?

[24]   The political is threatened insofar as man's dangerousness is threatened. Therefore the affirmation of the political is the affirmation of man's dangerousness. How should this affirmation be understood? Should it be intended *politically,* it can have "no normative meaning but only an existential meaning" (49), like everything political. One then will have to ask: in time of danger, in the "dire emergency," does "a fighting totality of men" affirm the dangerousness of its enemy? does it *wish for* dangerous enemies? And one will have to answer "no," along the lines of C. Fabricius's comment when he heard that a Greek philosopher had proclaimed pleasure as the greatest good: If only Pyrrhus and the Samnites shared this philosopher's opinion as long as we are at war with them! Likewise, a nation in danger wants its own dangerousness not for the sake of dangerousness, but for the sake of being rescued from danger. Thus, the affirmation of dangerousness as such has no political meaning but only a "normative," *moral* meaning; expressed appropriately, that affirmation is the affirmation of power as the power that forms states, of *virtù* in Machiavelli's sense. Here, too, we recall Hobbes, who describes fearfulness as the virtue (which, incidentally, is just as much negated by him as is the state of nature itself) of the state of nature, but who understands fearfulness as inclusive of glory and courage. Thus warlike morals seem to be the ultimate legitimation for Schmitt's affirmation of the political, and the opposition between the negation and the position of the political seems to coincide with the opposition between pacifist internationalism and bellicose nationalism.

[25]   Is that conclusion really correct? One has to doubt it if one considers the resolution with which Schmitt refuses to come on as a belligerent against the pacifists (33). And one must quarrel with the conclusion as soon as one has seen more precisely how Schmitt arrives at man's dangerousness as the ultimate presupposi-

tion of the position of the political. After he has aleady twice
rejected the pacifist ideal on the ground that the ideal in any case
has no meaning for behavior in the present situation and for the
understanding of this situation (36 f. and 54 f.), Schmitt—while
recognizing the possibility in principle of the "world state" as a
wholly apolitical "partnership in consumption and production" of
humanity united—finally asks "upon which men will the terrible
power devolve that a global economic and technical centralization
entails"; in other words, which men will *rule* in the "world state."
"This question cannot by any means be dismissed by hoping . . .
that government of men over men will have become superfluous,
because men will then be absolutely free; for the question immediately arises, *for what* they will be free. One can answer this question
with optimistic or pessimistic suppositions," namely with the optimistic supposition that man will then be undangerous, or with the
pessimistic supposition that he will be dangerous (58 f.). The question of man's dangerousness or undangerousness thus surfaces in
view of the question whether the government of men over men
is, or will be, necessary or superfluous. Accordingly, dangerousness
means *need of dominion.* And the ultimate quarrel occurs not between bellicosity and pacifism (or nationalism and internationalism) but between the "*authoritarian* and *anarchistic* theories" (60).

[26]   The quarrel between the authoritarian and the anarchistic theories concerns whether man is by nature evil or good.
But "evil" and "good," here, are "*not* to be taken in a specifically
moral or ethical sense" but are to be understood as "dangerous"
and "undangerous." What is thereby said becomes clear if one
takes into account the double meaning of "evil" that Schmitt mentions. "'Evil' can appear as corruption, weakness, cowardice, stupidity, *but also* as 'coarseness,' instinctual drivenness, vitality, irrationality, etc." (59). "Evil," in other words, can be understood either
as *human inferiority* or as *animal power,* as *humana impotentia* or
as *naturae potentia* (Spinoza, *Eth.* III *praef.*). Now if "evil" is not
meant in the moral sense, only the second meaning can be in

question here. In this sense "the philosophers of statecraft of the
seventeenth century (Hobbes, Spinoza, Pufendorff)" have described man in the state of nature as "evil": that is, "evil" "like
beasts that are moved by their drives (hunger, cupidity, fear, jealousy)" (59). But the question arises *why* these philosophers, Hobbes
in particular, understood man as "evil like the beasts." Hobbes
had to understand evil as *innocent* "evil" because he denied sin;
and he had to deny sin because he did not recognize any primary
obligation of man that takes precedence over every claim *qua* justified claim, because he understood man as by nature free, that is,
without obligation; for Hobbes, therefore, the fundamental political fact was natural right as the justified *claim* of the individual,
and Hobbes conceived of obligation as a *subsequent* restriction upon
that claim. If one takes this approach, one cannot demur in principle against the proclamation of human rights as claims of the
individuals upon the state and contrary to the state, against the
distinction between society and state, against liberalism—assuming
that liberalism is not altogether the unavoidable consequence of
the Hobbesian approach. And once one understands man's evil as
the innocent "evil" of the beast, but of a beast that can become
astute through injury and thus can be educated, the limits one sets
for education finally become a matter of mere *"supposition"*—
whether very narrow limits, as set by Hobbes himself, who therefore became an adherent of absolute monarchy; or broader limits such as those of liberalism; or whether one imagines education
as capable of just about everything, as anarchism does. The opposition between evil and good loses its keen edge, it loses its
very meaning, as soon as evil is understood as innocent "evil" and
thereby goodness is understood as an aspect of evil itself. The task
therefore arises—for purposes of the radical critique of liberalism
that Schmitt strives for—of nullifying the view of human evil as
animal and thus innocent evil, and to return to the view of human
evil as moral baseness; only in this way can Schmitt remain in
harmony with himself if indeed "the core of the political idea" is

"the *morally* demanding decision" (*Politische Theologie* 56). The correction that Schmitt undertakes in the view of evil held by Hobbes and his successors not only fails to meet the foregoing requirement but even contradicts it. Whereas in the case of Hobbes the natural and thus innocent "evil" is emphasized so that it can be *combated,* Schmitt speaks with an unmistakable *sympathy* of the "evil" that is not to be understood morally. This sympathy, however, is nothing other than *admiration* of animal power; and the same thing that Schmitt says in an already quoted passage on the aesthetic in general also applies to this admiration. Moreover, the inappropriateness of this sympathy immediately becomes clear when we discover that *what* is admired is not an excellence but a deficiency, a need (namely a need of dominion). Man's dangerousness, revealed as a need of dominion, can appropriately be understood only as moral baseness. It must be recognized as such, but it cannot be affirmed. But then what is the meaning of the affirmation of the political?

[27] *Why* Schmitt affirms the political, and, first of all, *that* he *affirms* it and does not merely recognize it as real or necessary, is shown most clearly in his polemic against the ideal that corresponds to the negation of the political. Ultimately Schmitt by no means repudiates this ideal as utopian—he says, after all, that he does not know whether it cannot be realized—but he does abhor it. That Schmitt does not display his views in a moralizing fashion but endeavors to conceal them only makes his polemic the more effective. Let us listen to Schmitt himself!: "if . . . the distinction between friend and enemy ceases even as a mere possibility, there will only be a politics-free weltanschauung, culture, civilization, economy, morals, law, art, *entertainment,* etc., but there will be neither politics nor state" (54). We have emphasized the word "entertainment" because Schmitt does everything to make entertainment *nearly* disappear in a series of man's serious pursuits; above all, the "etc." that immediately follows "entertainment" glosses over the fact that "entertainment" is really the ultimate

term in the series, its *finis ultimus*. Schmitt thus makes it clear: The opponents of the political may say what they will; they may appeal on behalf of their plan to the highest concerns of man; their good faith shall not be denied; it is to be granted that weltanschauung, culture, etc., do not *have* to be entertainment, but they *can* become entertainment; on the other hand, it is impossible to mention politics and the state in the same breath as "entertainment"; politics and the state are the only *guarantee* against the world's becoming a world of entertainment; therefore, what the opponents of the political want is ultimately tantamount to the establishment of a world of entertainment, a world of amusement, a world without *seriousness*. "A definitively pacified globe," Schmitt says in an earlier passage, "would be a world without politics. In such a world there could be various, perhaps *very interesting,* oppositions and contrasts, competitions and intrigues of all kinds, but no opposition on the basis of which it could sensibly be demanded of men that they sacrifice their lives" (35 f.; emphasis mine). Here, too, what Schmitt concedes to the pacifists' ideal state of affairs, what he *finds striking* about it, is its capacity to be interesting and entertaining; here, too, he takes pains to hide the criticism contained in the observation *"perhaps* very interesting." He does not, of course, wish to call into doubt whether the world without politics is interesting; if he is convinced of anything, it is that the apolitical world is *very* interesting ("competitions and intrigues of all sorts"); the "perhaps" only questions, but certainly *does* question, whether this capacity to be interesting can claim the interest of a human being worthy of the name; the "perhaps" conceals and betrays Schmitt's *nausea* over this capacity to be interesting, which is only possible if man has forgotten what genuinely matters. It thus becomes clear why Schmitt rejects the ideal of pacifism (more fundamentally: of civilization), why he affirms the political: he affirms the political because he sees in the threatened status of the political a threat to the seriousness of human life. The affirmation of the political is ultimately nothing other than the affirmation of the moral.

[28]   One reaches the same result if one looks more closely at Schmitt's description of the modern age as the age of depoliticization. With this description he certainly does *not* mean that in the nineteenth and twentieth centuries politics is to a less extent destiny than in the sixteenth and seventeenth centuries; today, no less than in earlier times, humanity is divided into "totalities that have a real possibility of fighting one another." A fundamental transformation has occurred, not in *the fact* that men quarrel but in *what* they quarrel *about*. What men quarrel about depends on what is considered important, authoritative. Different things are regarded as authoritative in different centuries: in the sixteenth century, theology was authoritative; in the seventeenth, metaphysics; in the eighteenth, morals; in the nineteenth, the economy; and in the twentieth, technology. Basically: in every century a different "domain" is the "central domain" (80–84). The political, because it has "no . . . domain of its own" (27), is never the "central domain." Whereas the "central domains" change, the political constantly remains destiny. But as *human* destiny the political is dependent upon what ultimately matters for man: "the state, too, [gets] its reality and power from the respective central domain, because the authoritative issues that groups, divided into friends and enemies, quarrel about are likewise determined by the authoritative domain" (86). The exact meaning of the depoliticization that is characteristic of the modern age can thus be discerned only if one understands which law rules in the "succession of changing central domains." This law is the "tendency toward neutralization," that is, the striving to gain a ground that "makes possible security, clarity, agreement, and peace" (89). Agreement and peace here mean agreement and peace at all costs. In principle, however, it is always possible to reach agreement regarding the means to an end that is already fixed, whereas there is always quarreling over the ends themselves: we are always quarreling with each other and with ourselves only over the just and the good (Plato, *Euthyphro* 7B–D and *Phaedrus* 263A). Therefore, if one seeks agreement at

all costs, there is no other path than to abandon entirely the question of what is right and to concern oneself solely with the means. It thus becomes intelligible that modern Europe, once it had started out—in order to avoid the quarrel over the right faith—in search of a neutral ground *as such,* finally arrived at faith in technology. "The self-evidence of today's widespread faith in technology is based only on the fact that people were able to believe that in technology they had found the absolutely and definitively neutral ground . . . In comparison to theological, metaphysical, moral, and even economic questions, which one can quarrel about forever, purely technical problems entail something refreshingly objective; they allow of solutions that are clear" (90). But the neutrality of technology is only apparent: "Technology always remains an instrument and a weapon, and precisely because technology serves everyone, it is not neutral" (90). The speciousness of this neutrality reveals the absurdity of the attempt to find an "absolutely and definitively neutral ground," to reach agreement at all costs. Agreement at all costs is possible only as agreement at the cost of the meaning of human life; for agreement at all costs is possible only if man has relinquished asking the question of what is right; and if man relinquishes that question, he relinquishes being a man. But if he seriously asks the question of what is right, the quarrel will be ignited (in view of "the inextricable set of problems" (90) this question entails), the life-and-death quarrel: the political—the grouping of humanity into friends and enemies—owes its legitimation to the seriousness of the question of what is right.

[29] The affirmation of the political is the affirmation of the state of nature. Schmitt opposes the affirmation of the state of nature to the Hobbesian negation of the state of nature. The state of nature is the *status belli,* pure and simple. Thus it appears that the affirmation of the state of nature can only be bellicose. That appearance fades away as soon as one has grasped what the return to the state of nature means for Schmitt. The affirmation of the state of nature does not mean the affirmation of war but "relin-

quishment of the security of the status quo" (93). Security is relinquished not because war would be something "ideal," but because
it is necessary to return from "splendid vicarage," from the "com-
fort and ease of the existing status quo" to the "cultural or social
nothing," to the "secret, humble beginning," "to undamaged, noncorrupt nature" (93) so that "out of the power of a pure and whole
knowledge . . . the order of the human things" can arise again
(95).

[30] If, then, according to Schmitt's actual opinion, the position of the political can be traced back to the position of the
moral, how does that position square with the polemic, which
pervades his whole text, against the primacy of morals over politics? The first explanation that suggests itself is that by "morals"
in that polemic he is referring to altogether specific morals, namely,
a morals that stands in fundamental contradiction to the political.
For Schmitt, "moral"—at least as used in the context here—
always refers to *"humanitarian* morality" (cf. 80 ff.). But that usage
means that Schmitt is tying himself to his opponents' view of
morality instead of questioning the claim of humanitarian-pacifist
morals to *be* morals; he remains trapped in the view that he is
attacking.

[31] Now the polemic against morals—against "ideals"
and "normative prescriptions"—does not prevent Schmitt from
passing a *moral* judgment on humanitarian morals, on the ideal of
pacifism. Of course, he takes pains, as we have shown, to conceal
this judgment. An *aporia* finds expression in this concealment: the
threatened status of the political makes necessary an evaluative
statement on the political; yet at the same time insight into the
essence of the political arouses doubt about all evaluative statements on the political. For such a statement would be a "free,
unmonitorable decision that concerns no one other than the person
who freely makes the decision"; it would essentially be a "private
matter" (49); but the political is removed from all arbitrary, private
discretion; it has the character of transprivate *obligation.* If it is

now presupposed that all ideals are private and thus nonobligatory, obligation cannot be conceived as such, as duty, but can be conceived only as inescapable necessity. It is this presupposition, then, that disposes Schmitt to assert the inescapability of the political, and—as soon as his subject matter forces him to stop maintaining this assertion—to conceal his moral judgment; and this presupposition is, as he himself emphasizes, the characteristic presupposition of the "individualistic-liberal society" (49).

[32]   Let us now make thoroughly clear what the affirmation of the political in disregard of the moral, the primacy of the political over the moral, would signify. Being political means being oriented to the "dire emergency." Therefore the affirmation of the political as such is the affirmation of fighting as such, wholly irrespective of *what* is being fought *for*. In other words: he who affirms the political as such comports himself *neutrally* toward all groupings into friends and enemies. However much this neutrality may differ from the neutrality of the man who denies the political as such, he who affirms the political as such and thereby behaves neutrally toward all groupings into friends and enemies does not want "to place" himself "outside the political totality . . . and live only as a private man" (52); he does not have the *will* to neutralization, to the avoidance of decision at all costs, but in fact is eager for decision; as eagerness for *any* decision *regardless of content,* this neutrality makes use of the possibility—which originally was made accessible for the sake of neutralization—of something that is beyond all decision. He who affirms the political as such respects all who want to fight; he is just as *tolerant* as the liberals—but with the opposite intention: whereas the liberal respects and tolerates all *"honest"* convictions so long as they merely acknowledge the legal order, *peace,* as sacrosanct, he who affirms the political as such respects and tolerates all *"serious"* convictions, that is, all decisions oriented to the real possibility of *war*. Thus the affirmation of the political as such proves to be a liberalism with the opposite polarity. And therewith Schmitt's statement that "the astonishingly consis-

tent . . . systematics of liberal thought" has "still not been replaced
in Europe today by any other system" (70) proves to be true.

[33] The affirmation of the political as such can therefore
be only Schmitt's first word against liberalism; that affirmation
can only *prepare for* the radical critique of liberalism. In an earlier
text Schmitt says of Donoso Cortés: he "despises the liberals,
whereas he respects atheistic-anarchistic socialism as his mortal
enemy . . ." (*Politische Theologie* 55). The battle occurs only between
mortal enemies: with total disdain—hurling crude insults or maintaining the rules of politeness, depending on temperament—they
shove aside the "neutral" who seeks to mediate, to maneuver,
between them. "Disdain" is to be taken literally; they do not deign
to notice the neutral; each looks intently at his enemy; in order
to gain a free line of fire, with a sweep of the hand they wave
aside—without looking at—the neutral who lingers in the middle,
interrupting the view of the enemy. The polemic against liberalism
can therefore only signify a concomitant or preparatory action: it
is meant to clear the field for the battle of decision between the
"spirit of technicity," the "mass faith that inspires an antireligious,
this-worldly activism" (93), and the opposite spirit and faith, which,
as it seems, still has no name. Ultimately, two completely opposed
answers to the question of what is right confront each other, and
these answers allow of no mediation and no neutrality (cf. the
remark about "two-membered antitheses" and "three-membered
diagrams" or "constructions" on p. 73). Thus what *ultimately* matters to Schmitt is not the battle against liberalism. For that very
reason the affirmation of the political as such is not his last word.
His last word is "the order of the human things" (95).

[34] It is nonetheless true that the polemic against liberalism very often seems to be Schmitt's last word, that he very often
gets entangled in the polemic against liberalism, and that he thus
gets diverted from his real intention and is detained on the level
staked out by liberalism. This entanglement is no accidental failure
but the necessary result of the principle that "all concepts of the

spiritual sphere . . . are to be understood only in terms of concrete political existence" (84), and that "all political concepts, ideas, and words" have "a *polemical* meaning" (31). *In concreto* Schmitt violates this principle, which itself is entirely bound to liberal presuppositions, by opposing his unpolemical concept of the state of nature to Hobbes's polemical concept of the state of nature; and he fundamentally rejects this principle by expecting to gain the order of human things from a *"pure and whole* knowledge" (95). For a pure and whole knowledge is never, unless by accident, polemical; and a pure and whole knowledge cannot be gained "from concrete political existence," from the situation of the age, but only by means of a return to the origin, to "undamaged, noncorrupt nature" (93).

[35]   We said [par. 14 above] that Schmitt undertakes the critique of liberalism in a liberal world; and we meant thereby that his critique of liberalism occurs in the horizon of liberalism; his unliberal tendency is restrained by the still unvanquished "systematics of liberal thought." The critique introduced by Schmitt against liberalism can therefore be completed only if one succeeds in gaining a horizon beyond liberalism. In such a horizon Hobbes completed the foundation of liberalism. A radical critique of liberalism is thus possible only on the basis of an adequate understanding of Hobbes. To show what can be learned from Schmitt in order to achieve that urgent task was therefore the principal intention of our notes.

INDEX OF NAMES